THE
GHOST
ARMY

THE GHOST ARMY

Conning the Third Reich

GERRY & JANET SOUTER

PICTURE CREDITS

Alamy: 46, 48, 97

Bernie Bluestein Collection: 7, 197, 200, 244

Getty Images: 21, 191

Imperial War Museum: 44, 84, 112, 155

National Archives and Records Administration, USA: 30, 130, 139, 182, 222, 228, 233

National Archives, United Kingdom: 38

Rick Beyer Collection: 246, 247

United States Army Signal Corps: 168

This edition published in 2019 by Arcturus Publishing Limited
26/27 Bickels Yard, 151–153 Bermondsey Street,
London SE1 3HA

AD005778UK

Printed in the UK

CONTENTS

For Bernie Bluestein, 603 Engineer, Camouflage Battalion, Special, 23rd Headquarters Special Troops 1944–1945, whose voice in these pages puts a face on steadfast courage, and for Frederic Fox, whose incredible unit diary is a lasting tribute to the trials and triumphs of the gallant 23rd.

"And after all, what is a lie?
'Tis but the truth in masquerade."
George Gordon, Lord Byron
(*Don Juan*, Canto XI)

"They Brought Show Business to World War II."
Colonel Harry L. Reeder, Commanding
Officer, 23rd Headquarters Special Troops

"Rarely, if ever, has there been a group of such a
few men, which had so great an influence on the
outcome of a major military campaign."
Top-Secret U.S. Army report

OVERTURE

The German MG 42 machine gun glowed blue-black with a soft film of dew beneath the full moon. Its muzzle pointed across a wide, deep meadow whose distant western edge ended at a dense wood that sprawled beneath a bed of lingering fog. The eastern edge of the woods facing the meadow was silent, despite the division of SS Panzer Grenadiers who crouched in the high grass among the fir trees, or peered from the hatches of their parked tanks, watching the fog. It was also silent farther back, where the woods thinned to a gentle slope and artillery crews knelt by their stock of shells in hard-edge moon shadows cast by their fearsome 88mm guns. An entire German division stood cocked and ready at the meadow's edge, poised to receive an attack. They listened.

Across the meadow, the arrogant Americans made no secret of their intentions. Sherman M4 tanks creaked and rumbled down the ridge line into position. No smokescreen or fog could hide that clanking sound, the guttural bursts of acceleration, gearshift clunks and whirring turret rotation. Listening hard by the meadow's edge, the Bavarian machine gunner could make out shouts in English as armour was directed to its assigned bombardment and jump-off stations. The cloying smell of petrol exhaust was on the breeze in the young Bavarian's face. He could taste it on his dry lips.

All day long, and for days previously, German radio monitors had listened in as the American armoured division had built up its force: tanks, half-tracks, trucks filled with men being directed here-and-there to assembly areas, water points or quartermaster stores. Aerial surveillance by a high-flying Fieseler Storch had brought back films of indifferently camouflaged tanks, artillery and a small airstrip for light reconnaissance aircraft. The German recon plane had barely made it through the anti-aircraft fire. Civilian agents left in the village to mingle with the Americans had brought back photographs of unit shoulder patches, jeep bumper stencils and signs – signs everywhere – even to the latrines, where all you had to do was follow your nose. The American armoured division was exactly where it was supposed to be – exactly where it was expected by the *Abwehr*, Germany's military intelligence bureau.

False dawn gradually turned the sky blue-grey and the MG 42 crew checked their ammunition belts for the tenth time, grabbed a bite of hoarded sausage and dark bread, checked the gun's breach and exercised cramped legs. They were coming. Eyes strained over open sights to find targets, dew dripped off helmets. Where were they?

An artillery shell dropped on their left, then another. Who was shooting? The entire left flank burst into smoke and flames. The machine-gun crew looked back at the empty field, revealed now as the fog burned off. German officers were shouting! The left flank bombardment swelled with the crescendo of close combat.

The Bavarian's crew began quickly dismantling the gun. A hurried fumble with ammo boxes and jingling cartridge belts, they scrambled from their dug-in position, their breath choked hot in their throats. The German gunner, cradling his slippery weapon in his arms, chanced a glance at the silent field stretching out behind him where an entire American armoured division had existed – and vanished – and reappeared miles away on his left flank. He was running now, trying to catch up to his crew. He left the phantoms behind – but kept glancing over his shoulder.

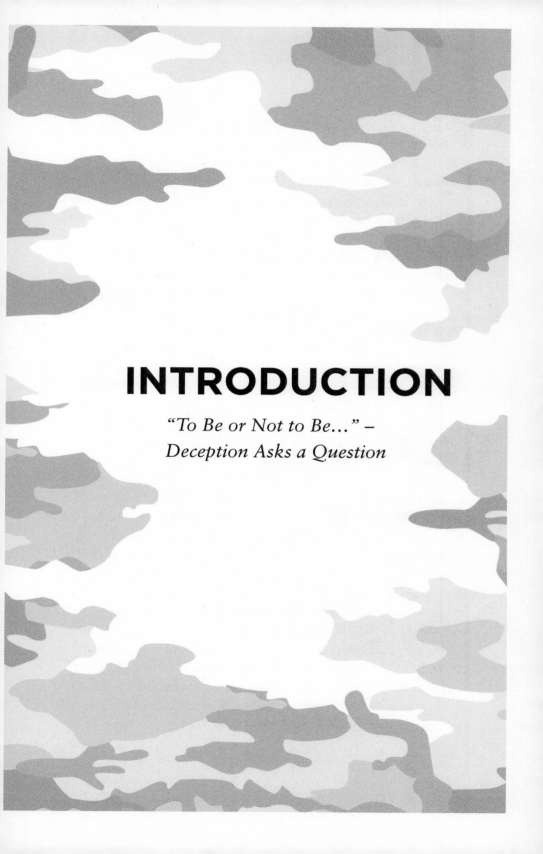

INTRODUCTION

"To Be or Not to Be…" –
Deception Asks a Question

Every nation that faced Adolf Hitler's army encountered a well-honed and battle-tested military machine. Constructed from the ashes of its World War I predecessor it was enveloped by an edge of fanaticism, whose political leaders were not averse to genocide and treachery in their pursuit of European dominance. As unprepared western nations faced its superior organization and will, implacable and devoid of empathy, they were pummelled into submission. It became obvious that an edge was needed to attack the twisted minds of the warlords who had built and steered this juggernaut. Its progress had to be slowed and misdirected. Time had to be purchased with guile and stealth. The free world weaponized its intellect and sent it off to war.

The critical edge proved to be deception, seasoned with a flair for the tactically theatrical. As the first German guns and bombs detonated, recovery began with the people of the British Isles. Their centuries-long experience of many forms of warfare had left them open to creative solutions on the battlefield, including imaginary and speculative deceits. Camouflage and duplicity with a dash of stagecraft would baffle the Germans and save thousands of lives in campaigns from North Africa and the Mediterranean to the invasion of Europe and onward into the very heart of Hitler's Third Reich.

Following victories in North Africa and the Mediterranean, the Allied armies used the British island fortress as the springboard to stage their attack on the European Theatre of Operations (ETO). They faced their most difficult challenge in hoodwinking the German High Command. To the complex menu of acronyms and code-names – OVERLORD, NEPTUNE, FORTITUDE, QUICKSILVER and FUSAG – they added an extra level of deceit. As the German commanders ensconced in their bunkers confidently expected a *Götterdämmerung*, the complete destruction of the Allies, the deceivers delivered instead a phantom invasion and a Ghost Army.

On 6 June 1944, Hitler's generals and intelligence chiefs scanned the coastline of Norway and the Pas-de-Calais for signs of the promised Allied invasion. Yet where were the landing craft that had dotted the British coast, rivers and estuaries? Where were the squadrons of bombers above the Atlantic Wall around Calais? Where was General Patton's hard-charging First United States Army Group?

The German High Command was confident. The flow of information from *Abwehr* agents and spies, and from aerial cameras overflying Britain had been constant and verified. The Nazi spy network's observations had confirmed the German generals' decisions. They deployed their Panzer armour and veteran battalions to precisely where the phantom illusionists had directed them, far from Normandy, the main combat arena.

Taken in by the Allied deceptions, Adolf Hitler had ordained that the Normandy invasion was a feint, a raid, a mere sideshow to suck in his precious reserves and drag his armies from their invincible concrete bunkers in the Pas-de-Calais. Even the most acute of German commanders, Field Marshal Erwin Rommel – the "Desert Fox" – was sufficiently taken in to spend 6 June – the very day of the Allied landings in Normandy – celebrating his wife's birthday at his home, the Villa Lindenhof in Baden-Württemberg, Germany.

The first act of the Allies' European campaign successfully battered its way across the sands of Normandy with grim, but acceptable results. The second and third acts pushed across France and the Low Countries until the final denouement at the banks of the River Rhine. Accompanying the Allied soldiers surging eastward across the European theatre of operations, was a small band of thespians, jesters, mountebanks and conjurers. These warrior wizards and master illusionists comprised the American 23rd Headquarters Specialty Troops, a 1,100-man composite command capable of successfully impersonating actual battalions, corps and whole armies. This was the Ghost Army.

When the end came in May 1945, the contribution of this phantom command vanished into the "CLASSIFIED TOP SECRET" files for 40 years. In a world of satellite imaging technology, computer-generated and monitored global communications and stealth weapons, the artifice and camouflage of the Ghost Army seem quaint historical artifacts. But today's digital wizardry stands on the shoulders of selected Tommies and GIs. The imagination and skills of these creatively gifted soldiers and academic boffins confounded the enemy and saved thousands of lives – both Allies and Germans – during the course of World War II. Our story is about the genesis and evolution of these phantoms and men-who-never-were, these artists and magicians at the front line who operated in stealth and secrecy. The accomplishments of the Ghost Army were buried in military archives until finally resurrected in literary re-telling four decades later. To aid in this telling, a member of the Ghost Army is still with us at age 95. Former Pfc Bernie Bluestein lends the voice of an artist-soldier to this amazing tale. And now at last, Bernie and the 23rd Headquarters Specialty Troops have been memorialized in 2018 with a monument erected in the European Theatre of World War II, an arena where they played their greatest roles and succeeded in conning Adolf Hitler.

CHAPTER 1

A LEGACY
OF STEALTH

The start of World War II in the British Isles found the British Expeditionary Force (BEF) with no official camouflage policy. There was no shortage of studies: there were schemes where airfields were painted over to not look like airfields; house rooftops were painted on those of war industry buildings; Royal Navy destroyers and cruisers were geometrically daubed with grey, blue and white zig-zag "dazzle paint" to try and break up their outlines. Millions of gallons of paint came to virtually nothing, but the dog's breakfast of schemes did attract many curious artists and designers to enquire at recruiting offices and offer their services.

Among these artists was Freddie Beddington, a 43-year-old former art student, who had attended the Slade School of Art after service in World War I. His sharp shooting eye saw him serving as a sniper, lying silent beneath a rumpled leaf-stick-and-grass tuft-suit of his own design, invisible in the Flanders mud, picking off Germans. Nature had been his guide to concealment, observing the sun-spot speckled deer, the many-hued chameleon lizard, and insects who imitated predators or hid in plain sight as tree bark and green sticks.

His college days had put him in touch with many artists and designers. At the outbreak of yet another war, Beddington presented himself at the War Office. To his surprise, he was elevated to the position of Camouflage Advisor to the BEF Engineer-in-Chief in France. His job was to recruit artists into the war business. His older brother Jack was already in the creative film-making field, shooting commercial work for Shell-Mex and BP. His artistic contacts were natural recruits for Freddie's newly formed Camouflage Training and Development Centre.[1]

About the same time, Geoffrey de Gruchy Barkas entered the scene. Another former World War I veteran, he met Jack Beddington while filming for Shell-Mex. Barkas was making a good living as a film maker and was excited about the prospects of doing the same with the BEF. He signed up, hoping for a speedy assignment to film for the war effort. Instead, he was dumped into the Permit Branch of the Postal and Telegraph Censorship Department, where he languished as a paper-pusher.

On 1 September 1939, at 4.45 a.m., Germany invaded Poland. Britain, who had pledged to defend the Poles, declared war on Germany two days later. On the Western Front, however, there was little immediate action and the "Phoney War" had land armies facing each other for eight months, waiting for something to break up the boredom. Barkas, desperate to get out of his desk job, called Jack Beddington for help. Beddington, who was now cranking out British war propaganda films, mentioned his brother Freddie's Camouflage Centre might be worth a try. Barkas grasped this straw and asked for

Propaganda film maker Jack Beddington – shown with movie star, Rosalind Russell – along with his artist brother, Freddie, helped promote camouflage to priority status in the military arsenal.

an audition with Beddington's brother. Instead of Freddie, Barkas sat down in front of Captain Richard M. Buckley.

Buckley was a decorated World War I veteran and fellow film-maker. He seemed curiously unimpressed with Barkas' biography, but instead went off on a promotion of camouflage needs for the coming conflict. Film-maker Barkas left the interview unclear about his chances of landing any kind of work filming for the war effort.

As if this intertwining of artistic types was not complex enough, another character joined the cast. Jasper Maskelyne, a stage magician with some reputation for card and rope tricks, sleight-of-hand and mind-reading mysteries, had been riding high in 1936. However, his next year's tour had grown stale and flopped, leaving him short of funds, so he offered himself to the War Office. Using his personal magnetism and banter about his on-stage illusions, he managed to secure an interview with Captain Buckley. Though Buckley was amused by the patter of this obviously ego-driven con man, he wondered, if Maskelyne could make a girl vanish on stage, what could he do with a Churchill Tank?

The magician believed he had a future in camouflage, when he was whisked off to the Royal Engineers' Camouflage Training and Development Centre at Farnham Castle. In this ancient pile dating back to 1138, his classmates included the British artists Roland Penrose, Stanley William Hayter and Julian Trevelyan. Maskelyne found the training exercises boring and longed for his calling: making things disappear in front of appreciative audiences – or in this case, baffled Nazis. Out on the camouflage field, however, the magician's legerdemain was found wanting when it came to making pill boxes or lorries go away. His attempted illusions were far more grandiose – if often impractical: battleships, air fields and the Suez Canal.

As the war progressed, Maskelyne was shipped off to Cairo to serve in MI9, a branch of military intelligence dedicated to assisting Allied prisoners of war and resistance networks, under the command of Brigadier Dudley Clarke. The master magician was put in charge of developing hidden escape gadgets for British prisoners of war: wire-cutters hidden in cricket bats; saws in combs; and playing cards containing tiny escape maps.

Geoffrey Barkas had already met Maskelyne and many other artists, illustrators, designers, sculptors, art directors and architects, including Trevelyan and Penrose from the Royal Engineers at Larkhill back in England. Now, he was unpacking at Napier Barracks in Kent for the No. 2 Camouflage Course. Here he would undergo the buckled-up reality of military training. He and his fellow artists were reminded the war was real by watching newsreels of German General Rommel chasing French Army and BEF remnants back toward the sea. Learning to hide things from the enemy seemed counterproductive in stopping the Nazi tide, but their training would change that equation. Their rumpled, Bohemian days were behind them and creativity took on a different meaning now they had accepted the King's shilling.

In the classrooms, they learned to apply light, shade, colour and texture to practical deception needs. Homely bales of netting became camouflage in creative hands. Landscapes were examined closely, not for composition or beauty, but for their ability to hide a tank, a supply dump or a band of *camoufleurs* beneath a storm of Nazi artillery or Luftwaffe bombs. Their grades were measured in estimated lives saved, and battle-hardened enemy troops baffled or rooted in place. The students learned that armies carve a wide swath in the countryside when they move. You can hear an army long before it reaches you, smell an army's encampment, see an army's tell-tale path over ground in tyre and tank treads and spot supply and field headquarters in aerial photographs.

Camouflage can become a stealth weapon – often showing the enemy what he expects to see, convincing him what he has heard from spies is true, and that what he has seen in photographs is also true. The students watched films made of the history of camouflage and misinformation, of hoaxes and decoys dating back to the

Carthaginians and the American Civil War's Stonewall Jackson, each of whom built fake field camps to inflate the size of his army.

What they also learned was that the creative skills they brought to their training and their natural gifts were not to be used for their work's aesthetic beauty and exquisite craftmanship, but to create a false reality, a composite of lies. The battlefield is a blunt, mundane, deadly place where survival is based on recognizing danger, seeking places of safety, and defending your ground when threatened. Bravery, courage and attacking are all cultural constructs imposed by pre-conditioning and bursts of adrenalin. Redirecting, channelling, or confounding the enemy's cultural pre-conditioning is a learned skill and produces a satisfying burst of creativity.

Except for villages far from the war zones, the battlefield's palette is monochrome: armies in olive drab and field grey, weapons in shades of green, burnt umber, sienna, metallic blue and shell-casing brass. Houses and buildings crumble in rubble brown, brick red, dirty cement and exposed wallpaper. Civilian dead sprawl in dark doorless doorways, or litter scorched fields among black and brown horse corpses after a saturation bombing. In addition to natural surroundings, this was the palette of war.

As expected in the North African desert battlefield, sand coloured the landscape, coloured the uniforms, coloured the faces and the weapons, coloured the trucks and lorries, the tanks and aircraft. That combat zone would be a graduation master class for the performers of camouflage and deception.

With teeth-grinding acceptance, the artists in the No. 2 Camouflage Course stuffed themselves into khaki, belted with webbing, and ordered into straight lines. They endured humiliation at the hands of professional drill-sergeants, but could not suppress their need to exercise their core gifts. During lectures, they sketched and they drew. In their spare time, they painted, sculpted and played with materials at hand. They wrote in journals and diaries and cartooned in the margins. The *camoufleurs* kept the grey cells limber and that made them valuable to a monolithic, monochromatic army. They thought and schemed, becoming confidence tricksters among their own officers and learned the elements of the long con which they would need to scam the Germans. They looked creatively at life and the mundane, mud-speckled world they would inherit and considered, "What can we do to really mess up the Nazis and not get shot – by either side?"

One afternoon, Barkas was returning to barracks, relishing the beautiful English countryside, when he paused near a road crossing as a line of soldiers passed. These marchers, no, these *stragglers* shuffled past, no weapons, no strut, no eye contact; their uniforms looked borrowed. Those without shirts or battle jackets were draped with filthy creased rags held in place by habit. Some

The creative art of camouflage was put to good use in North Africa – this tracked vehicle is masquerading as a truck.

had helmets, most didn't; almost all carried lazaret bags handed out by the Red Cross. These men had seen death and defeat, had experienced despair, and now were back home from the evacuation of Dunkirk's bloody beaches in June 1940. Barkas' clean uniform, polished leather and shined shoes seemed almost shameful as the last of the column passed down the slope that led to a distant barracks.

Geoffrey Barkas also felt humbled by his artist colleagues, all useful and skilled craftsmen able to conjure weapons of war from bits of rubber, string and a red sable brush. His contribution seemed as diaphanous as their concealing smoke screens, easily torn apart by a breeze. He was stunned when he awoke on 4 July 1940 to find himself rostered as a second lieutenant. Before he could locate a pair of shoulder boards for his uniform, mid-day found him re-rostered as a first lieutenant, and by tea time, he shouldered his duffle wearing captain's boards and accompanied by his very own staff lieutenant, his friend Michael Bell.

They were both on their way to Northern Ireland to teach the army how to hide its stuff. Barkas learned the army could move like lightning when its skids were properly greased. Through the incessant prodding and convincing of the Beddington brothers and Buckley, camouflage had been notched up a bit in priority. Now, Barkas and Bell had to become salesmen, not pushing vacuum cleaners or encyclopedia sets, but converting a broad base of influential traditional army officers into Camouflage Believers.

To an Old Guard army playing catch-up with the Germans, allocating funds, labour and time to a bunch of unarmed civilian sign-painters, radio-frequency fiddlers, backstage showrunners, rubber-balloon inflators and noise makers who couldn't even throw a decent salute was a waste of valuable resources. To the unconvinced, camouflage meant tossing a net over a cannon, parking a tank next to a barn, sticking a shrub in your helmet band and making quite sure the mademoiselle you were romancing wasn't a Nazi spy. All the rest of the military effort went to feed the god of fire and manoeuvre.

To combat this entrenched philosophy, Barkas had one basic, irrefutable argument – delivered with a smile, of course – "Hide it, or die." His demonstrations – aimed at the highest-level command he could round up – made a forceful point. Using borrowed troops and vehicles supposedly "camouflaged," he had a light aircraft armed with flour-sack bombs buzz over the thinly forested field to "bomb" anything suspicious or not native to the area. Later, while the Tommies were brushing flour out of their hair and lorry drivers busied themselves brooming off the flour-white roofs of their not-so hidden vehicles, the implied casualty count was driven home.[2]

To help overcome the army's casual attitude to camouflage, Barkas called up his muse and produced a pamphlet on the subject that included an "instructional poem" titled "The Sad Story of George Nathaniel Glover". Glover was a driver who "never, never could be made to Park his Lorry in The Shade" and who uses a net "Which he had thrown across the bonnet With not a stitch of garnish on it". As a result, the bomb falls exactly on target and when his friends come to find him, "Not One Trace did they discover of Driver George Nathaniel Glover."

The pamphlet became a best seller, spreading throughout British commands in all theatres. A book would follow, titled *Concealment in the Field,* which became another camouflage classic. For the most part, Barkas' teaching in classes and lecturing in the officers' club stuck to advice given him by Buckley to "make things up as he went along". Film producers or showrunners must think on their feet and know a bit about every member of the crew they are supposed to manage. For Geoffrey Barkas, though he lacked hands-on skills of the artist-craftsman-composer-designer, he knew how to use those skills to form a team to create a convincing camouflage, or a "notional" world that the Nazis would accept. Soon, he was moved into his headquarters in Farnham Castle in Surrey, whose medieval remains dated from a time when fortifications were valued more than fakery and camouflage.

This final chapter in Barkas' training saga was cut short in November 1940 when the international situation in North Africa had Barkas packing up to leave for Cairo along with his team. Departing from Liverpool Docks, he would not see Natalie, his wife of 15 years, for another two years. He sailed aboard the *Andes* in an escorted convoy in which every passenger did his part. Barkas manned a Bofors ack-ack gun for the voyage, but saw no U-boats. He and his troupe of sorcerers, poseurs and mountebanks must have felt naked afloat on the flat sea with not a deception solution in sight. Their arrival in the Sahara Desert would do nothing to allay those fears.

Barkas quickly hooked a ride in a Lysander recon aircraft for a look at the colours in the North African landscape in order to play out his deception strategy. Expecting to see tans, umbers, mustard and tertiary variables, he was surprised by the variations in landscape. Wind-eroded mountains, lush swampy valleys and outcroppings of upthrust volcanic basalt broke up the endless dunes below. He had learned to think in terms of the manoeuvring of tanks and other treaded machines, of four- and six-wheeled lorries. His aerial surveillance instead revealed fields of quick sand. Where camels could trek easily on padded hooves, a Cruiser tank would sink up past its fitfully churning bogies.

Once arrived in Egypt, Barkas established his "Camouflage Development and Training Camp" at Helwan, on the banks of the Nile, in January 1942. To study the flora and fauna of the vast Sahara, he added zoologist Hugh B. Cott to serve as his chief instructor. The expansion of Barkas' authority in the British Middle East Command surprised him, as he realized the concept of camouflage had been accepted as an essential element for every army unit – a strategic as well as a tactical weapon of war. With that additional authority came yet another promotion to the rank of lieutenant-colonel.[3]

To both justify and drive home the importance of properly set up camouflage to the Middle East Command, Barkas called upon Steve

Sykes, one of his officers, to divert Italian bombers from attacking the railhead at Capuzzo where materials were being delivered for Operation CRUSADER, intended to break the Axis siege of Tobruk. Sykes, a Royal Engineers survivor of Dunkirk and student of stained-glass art at the Royal College of Art, had joined the Camouflage Unit at Farnham Castle after being recruited by Richard Buckley. He immediately grasped the Capuzzo railhead problem when asked by Brigade Commander Robertson, "How are you going to hide this lot then?"

Sykes suggested a dummy railhead at distant Misheifa, complete with a dummy nine-mile rail line ending at a terminal with sidings and buildings – most of them still under construction – which would imply to Axis observers that the start of CRUSADER was being delayed. On gaining approval, Sykes discovered there was not enough lumber to build his creation. After seeing aerial photos of the area from different altitudes he decided to scale the whole railway down to two-thirds life size.[4]

Using woven palm fronds as his primary building material and empty gas cans hammered into rail shapes for the track, and by considering the desert haze and distortion of size and perspective offered by the otherwise featureless desert, the illusion worked.

As the phoney railroads practically begged to be bombed, the Italian air force obliged and dropped over 100 bombs on the Misheifa line and railhead. After the Italians fled North Africa on 13 May 1943, one of their maps of the area was found to have the Misheifa railhead clearly marked as destroyed by aerial bombing. Later on, the Commander-in-Chief of the Eighth Army, Lieutenant-General Neil Ritchie, sent Sykes a message:

"To G 2 Cam: Will you please convey to all those concerned in the construction and maintenance of the Dummy R[ail] H[ead] my congratulations on the success which the scheme has achieved ... Neil Ritchie, Lt. Gen. GOC-in-C Eighth Army"[5]

Steven Sykes would miss working with Geoffrey Barkas

Dummy tanks were used with great success in confusing German intelligence. They made it seem as if the Allies had more tanks than they actually did, and they also diverted attention away from where the real tanks were. Here, British troops inflate a rubber dummy tank in 1940.

on Operation BERTRAM, the upcoming British camouflage masterpiece, due to illness and exhaustion. However, his theories and practices were essential to that operation and the subsequent defeat of General Erwin Rommel's Afrika Korps in North Africa. Barkas later described as, "... the task of providing props for the biggest 'film production' on which I ever expect to be engaged".[6]

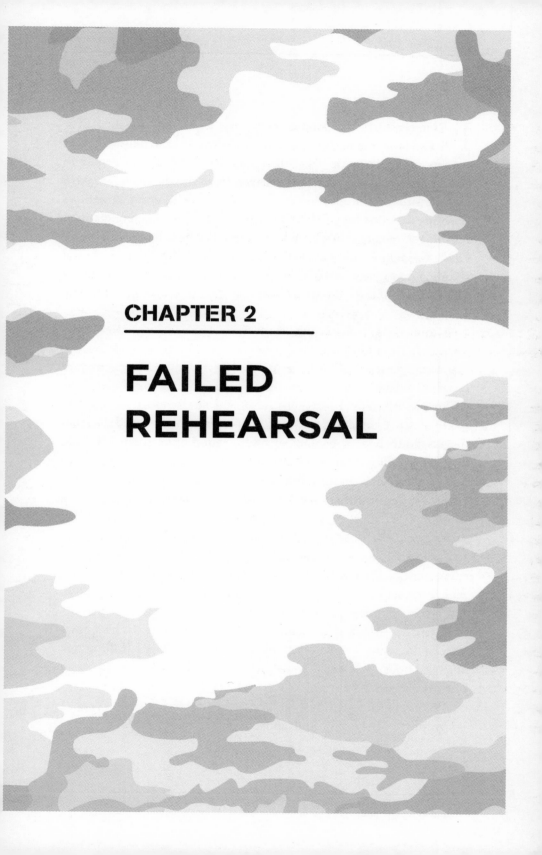

CHAPTER 2

FAILED REHEARSAL

Nineteen forty-two loomed bleak and forbidding for the Allies. The Japanese had crushed the Americans in the Philippines, at Bataan and Corregidor. The British had won the battle of Britain in the air, but their army had been driven from the shores of Dunkirk and the situation in North Africa was at a tipping point. America's previous material help for the British had thinned out since Japan's crushing December 1941 raid on Pearl Harbor. In the spring of 1942, Germany's submarine war was sweeping the Atlantic of vital shipping and Hitler had overrun France in a lightning blitz of tanks and mobile infantry. Politically and strategically, the Allied global position was a mess.

Britain was still reeling from the effects of the Blitz (the Luftwaffe's bombing campaign against British cities) and lived in fear of Operation SEALION, Hitler's projected invasion of the south coast. Civilians continued to dig casualties out of rubble and the authorities attempted to reconstitute vital industries. Evacuees fled from ruined population centres and strategic targets, and a black-market flourished in the pace of severe rationing of food and other necessities. But in spite of all these setbacks, the desire for vengeance against the Nazis burned hot among civilian and military voices raised on street corner soap boxes and in sandbagged planning rooms.

In 1942, the Allies still lacked the combat and transport strength to launch a full cross-Channel invasion (as they would ultimately carry out in Operation OVERLORD in 1944). Instead, British planners cast about for a rehearsal for the planned main assault. They settled on the French coastal town of Dieppe near Pas-de-Calais, where the English Channel is at its narrowest. This choice also fit in with OVERLORD planning for the large-scale attack against Hitler's "Atlantic Wall", which was still in the early stages of construction.

The intelligence gathered on the enemy preparations and Dieppe's geography, topography and shore defences was wanting: tourist holiday maps showed the beach's gradient as being acceptable for crossing with massed troops and tanks, but not its composition. Aerial photographs failed to identify sighted gun bunkers cut into low vertical cliffs facing the beach, leaving landing troops exposed to enfilading fire. In addition to these failures of British intelligence, the Germans had been warned by their own network of French double agents that the British were unusually fixated on Dieppe. Lousy security precautions along Britain's south coast also flooded the airwaves with increased radio traffic which was driving the movements of heavy amphibious units.

On the morning of 19 August, British torpedo boats scouting the offshore landing area were engaged by a patrol of German gunboats off Puys and Berneval, ruining all attempts at secrecy. Counting on shock value, the force slammed ashore.

The Dieppe Raid was a flop. Virtually everything that had been planned went wrong; some by bad luck, but most through bad intelligence. Everywhere, it seemed, the Axis powers were winning victory after victory. Somewhere – anywhere – they had to be stopped by strength, by stealth, by God – or by sneakiness.

CHAPTER 3

PUTTING ON THE MED - DECEPTIONS AT EL ALAMEIN

Lieutenant-Colonel Dudley Clarke was one of those square pegs that didn't quite fit into the British Army's round hole. He was a brilliant tactician and had created the Commandos – highly trained, very tough and stealthy – for raids and work behind enemy-lines. He did have a few quirks. Ordered to Spain as part of an espionage operation, he was arrested by the Spanish police; not for undercover secret message passing, but for dressing as a woman. He claimed that his frock, along with his pert hat perched upon his coiffure, purse and high heels, was a disguise. Versions of this excuse eventually freed him.

As the battle in North Africa wore on in 1942, the British Eighth Army commanded by Gen. Claude Auchinleck, continued a slow and cautious advance, well supplied as it flogged the third-rate

Brigadier General Dudley Clarke – also shown here in spy craft female disguise – was a talented and eccentric leader, and a pioneer of military deception in North Africa. He conceived "A-Force" intelligence gathering and British Commandos, who became today's vaunted Special Air Service (SAS).

Code-breakers working at Bletchley Park were instrumental in the war effort using the Enigma-code-breaking computer "Colossus".

Italians. Now, they faced German General Erwin Rommel – the "Desert Fox" – and his audacious tactics, better armour, and the hard, loyal troops of his Afrika Korps. But the British interdiction of his supply-line meant that Rommel was subject to rationing of ammunition and fuel. Auchinleck also had a secret weapon in his arsenal. Back in England, code-breakers working at the secret government cryptography establishment at Bletchley Park in Buckinghamshire had cracked the German code sent from Enigma machines, pre-war coding devices adapted for military use which the Nazis believed were absolutely secure. The British called the translated German intercepted messages ULTRA and were able to read a high proportion of the wireless messages the Germans sent.

Auchinleck needed a fortnight to prepare for Rommel's inevitable offensive. He sent for Dudley Clarke and his "A-Force" team to stall the Desert Fox. Clarke's A-Force was a deception department he had set up in Cairo at the request of General Archibald Wavell, commander of North African forces at the outbreak of war. Clarke was tasked with deceiving the Germans with any means possible to take maximum use of meagre British defences. Lacking actual combat assets, Clarke had to use his A-Force to cobble together a phantom, or "ghost army" where none existed.

Given those limited resources, Clarke planted a mix of false radio transmissions about luring the Afrika Korps onto Auchinleck's mine field – the last gasp of an under-strength army. Clarke also brewed-up a phoney troop disposition map "lost from Auchinleck's headquarters" which he had placed in a staged scout car wreck. The "wreck" was conveniently found by a German patrol and taken to Rommel who was convinced and delighted that Auchinleck was about to make his exhausted "last stand" on the Alam Halfa ridge near the El Alamein railway station. Seizing on this chance for a quick victory, Rommel unloaded his entire command on an overwhelming offensive thrust at the supposed collapsing British.

Aided by Clarke's bait and those secret ULTRA transmission intercepts of German coded wireless orders, Auchinleck was waiting. His troops rose up from camouflaged positions with a crash of artillery, and a churning line of tanks supported by infantry. The Nazi offensive was blunted. Confused and retreating, the Afrika Korps fell under strafing Hurricane fighters and twin-engine Boston bombers. Bogged-down half-tracks and precious Panzer armour lay slewed across the impassable bog called the Qattara Depression. In all, the Germans lost 50 tanks, 70 guns and – hardest on the Afrika Korps morale – 4,800 men. This confrontation was later named the First Battle of El Alamein. The Second Battle would be more gruelling still, but with a new commander, General Bernard Law Montgomery.

The El Alamein railway station became the focal point for the following, all-or-nothing battle. Montgomery knew that Rommel knew he was coming. Rommel predicted Montgomery was planning a numerically overwhelming offensive that would take forever to prepare, but when it fell, the blow would be crushing. What Rommel didn't know was the critical pieces of information: *when* the British were coming and from *what direction*. For the direction, there were only two choices: from the north or the south.

Dudley Clarke and his A-Force of ghost army operatives once again went to work. From his creative, theatrical mind, the plot emerged in three parts. The strategic part was code-named TREATMENT, feeding false wireless intelligence to the Wehrmacht that the British planned to attack the island of Crete. The second deception, Operation CANTWELL, used 25 radio transmitters posing as the Eighth Army Tactical Headquarters and the communication centre for the movements of a corps, two divisions and five brigades. Thirdly, the decoy and camouflage business fell to BERTRAM, creating the visual illusion that Monty's army would be attacking from the south and not north. Clarke sketched out the broad strokes before he was reassigned back to England to help plan Operation TORCH – the American invasion of North Africa and HUSKY, the amphibious landings on Sicily.

His rough draft for TREATMENT was turned over to Colonel Harry Noel Havelock Wild – going by the handle, Noel Wild – while Lieutenant-Colonel Charles Richardson took over BERTRAM. Wild was Clarke's friend and became second-in-command of Operations in the A-Force, working in Cairo producing false wireless intelligence for Rommel's commanders. The 34-year-old Richardson was a survivor of Dunkirk and had spent a year in Cairo with the Special Operations Executive (SOE) as part of Clarke's A-Force. He became overall planner for BERTRAM.

The Eighth Army counter-offensive was expected and the Afrika Korps, smarting from its humiliation at First El Alamein, was acutely sensitive to even the most miniscule attempt at British deception. When Germany rushed to Libya to rescue the Italians, Rommel found himself on the wrong side of the logistics war. Until reinforcements arrived, he was lacking in tanks, artillery, infantry, virtually everything he needed to battle General Archibald Wavell's British force that had just pounded Italian General Graziani's army flat at Beda Fomm. Instead of waiting for his full complement of panzers, Rommel pressed ahead. He inflated the size of his force by creating a ghost army of his own; having tanks haul bunches of desert bushes across ridge lines to make huge dust clouds, thus faking squadrons of panzers. He doubled the size of his armour running through villages, looping the parade around to pass through again. Armour on the move by rail was augmented by canvas-covered fake tanks and half-tracks on flat cars, rolling in long processions. His movements were clouded by fake radio traffic. Wavell bought the ghost deceptions and hesitated long enough for Rommel's real reinforcements to arrive and then the hound became the hare, and the British found themselves fighting for their lives.

This made Clarke's task even more difficult. BERTRAM covered a variety of battlefield sleights-of-hand supporting the northern offensive thrust scheduled for the night of 23 October beneath a full moon. The Germans had to be made to believe that Monty's main thrust would arrive across the southern approaches no earlier than 7 November.

Montgomery's Chief of Staff, Brigadier-General Francis "Freddie" de Guingand laid out the situation for the Middle East Camouflage Department:

"Well, there it is. You must conceal 150,000 men with 1,000 guns and a thousand tanks on a plain as flat and hard as a billiard table, and the Germans must not know a thing about it, although they will be watching every movement, listening for every noise, charting every track. You can't do it, of course, but you've bloody well got to."

Dudley Clarke had turned to Lieutenant-Colonel Geoffrey Barkas and his band of camouflage artists for the physical deceptions. Meanwhile, Clarke's "A-Force" code and wireless interceptors had scooped up Rommel's source of local intelligence code-named "Kondor", who was operating out of Cairo. British operators learned Kondor's cipher system, which used passages from Daphne de Maurier's novel, *Rebecca*, and proceeded to conjure up all manner of bogus "secret intelligence" to feed to him.

Barkas had 30 days to achieve the impossible – turning a battleground into a stage set under Rommel's critical eye, ear and nose for fakery and his *Fingerspitzengefühl* – the intuition in his fingertips. One of the great problems of producing deceptions that fool the enemy is like that of a magician explaining to his audience how his tricks are performed. The second time around, they know what to look for. Deceptions, ghosts and illusions had become a part of the North African battlefield. They were expected by both sides – each daring the other to untangle the real from the fraud. The basic aim of BERTRAM was to keep the armour on Rommel's southern wing – half of his total force – planted there. Rommel must never know that Montgomery's X Corps had instead been parked behind XXX Corps facing the northern jump-off. All Rommel must see was a giant harmless lorry park facing his northern positions.

The actual preparation for the BERTRAM deception began on 26 September. Barkas gathered his camouflage team starting with Tony Ayrton, Majors R.J. Southron, V.W. Hampton, Captain Philip Cornish and Lieutenants Brian Robb and Sidney Robinson. Added to these were three Pioneer companies (made up of skilled labourers and dummy-makers) headed by stage magician Jasper Maskelyne. These were, in turn fortified by paid native labour in Cairo and Alexandria who fashioned dummies and props for the various parts of BERTRAM. From these "factories" came dummy tanks, "sunshield" tank covers, dummy lorries, dummy cannon, millions of "gun flashes" and thousands of "Chinese" cloth soldiers. Due to the absolute secrecy, none of the civilian workers built complete dummies – only parts which were then assembled by the men of Jasper's "Magic Gang".

This seemingly parked truck used in Operation BERTRAM in North Africa (October 1942) is actually a Crusader Tank. The outer cover splits in half and is removed when the tank goes into action.

Shifting supply bases from north to south was the most critical illusion – especially with the 6,000 tons of resources needed by the northern attacking force near El Alamein. To offset this logistical nightmare, Colonel Barkas was handed an unexpected gift.

Ayrton and Robb discovered 100 sections of slit trench lined with concrete masonry that had become part of the desert landscape. By adding 2,000 tons of rectangular fuel cans as fake "facing" to the masonry trench-lining, the aerial signature of the trench was virtually unchanged, but the canned fuel was instantly accessible to the northern army and Montgomery's tanks. Intermittent RAF flyovers proved the illusion worked.

Hiding and transporting an immense quantity of ammunition,

food and other stores in crates and boxes was the next test. Stacking these boxes in the approximate shape of three-ton trucks "hidden" under loose canvas was Brian Robb's brainchild. The supply dump looked like a common military lorry park and not dangerous. Scattering real lorries driving around the park added to the trickery. Soldiers' "bivvies" (tents) were scattered about the park to conceal more supplies.

Artillery was another matter. Two guns dove-tailed together with their ammunition limbers formed a compact shape when covered with a canvas framework supported by poles that literally "swallowed" the identity of the artillery. The four wheels of the two guns added to the illusion of truck mobility. This shape resembled another badly camouflaged truck and earned the name "Cannibal".

Tanks and other armour presented a greater challenge. Some had to be mobile after their camouflage was applied in order to roll along in columns, or scuttle about in fake tank parks. Mobility was accomplished by fitting a metal framework in the skeleton shape of a Crusader or Sherman tank over a Jeep or other small utility vehicle and shaping out the illusion with canvas made to fit. Even light machine guns could be mounted, but the vehicle had to be stopped to man these weapons. Top speed was only about 10 mph (16 km/h) for the two-man crew.

Using canvas and wood, a clamshell-like hood Maskelyne called a "Sunshield" was fashioned that could fit over an armoured vehicle's working parts, turning a tank or half-track into another harmless "lorry". The actual Sherman, Grant, Churchill, Crusader or Valentine tanks and half-tracks were moved 60 miles (100 kilometres) behind the fake northern jump-off line – obviously too far away for serious attack consideration. The "Sunshield" armour – 700 of them – were placed in an innocuous lorry park just behind the northern jump-off where Montgomery's 1st and 10th Armoured Divisions had been expected.

All Rommel's aerial reconnaissance pilots saw was a heavy

Creating a desert parade of decoy lorries, cobbled together from canvas, paint and sticks looks convincing enough in German aerial photographs.

concentration of armour well away from the north. The BERTRAM team also figured that if Rommel sensed some of the near-by northern "lorries" were fakes, he would assume that the main attack would come from the south. This troubling thought nagged him, because the northern approach was the logical, most obvious, easiest launch point for Montgomery's attack. Had predictable Monty suddenly become "tricky"? Since his surprise drubbing at the first battle of El Alamein, Rommel felt uneasy. He could not afford another thrashing. One more failure would mean the loss of confidence of his most important backer, Adolf Hitler.

Meanwhile, the masterpiece of BERTRAM was created around water needed for the harsh desert. When preparations began in September, Barkas' team discovered a shallow-buried water pipeline already running from the El Imayid train station to a point behind El Alamein. Using a magician's trick of misdirection, Army Troops Company 578 extended a dummy addition to the actual pipeline. This new pipe inched its way south toward a southern location at

Samaket Gaballa to supply the notional Eighth Army. The operation was named DIAMOND. This fake pipe made of empty fuel cans was laid in a trench at the rate of five miles (eight kilometres) per day. At night, it was emptied of cans and filled in with sand by hundreds of soldiers. The trenching operation moved to begin slogging away with the same cans toward the south at sunrise. To enhance the deception, three dummy pumping stations, can-filling stations and a rather large reservoir were erected along the route – "serviced" by real tank trucks adding to the lorry tyre-marks showing Luftwaffe aerial cameras a busy enterprise underway.[7]

As this pipeline crept across the desert, it was obvious the work would not be completed until early November – the month fed to Rommel by his spies in Cairo who had been replaced by British A-Force code masters. The impression of Monty's sluggishness was reaffirmed. To further seed the impression of the southern front at Munassib as the launch point, BERTRAM planted a scattering of real troops moving about and built fake administration huts, field kitchens and a massive storage dump large enough to hold 9,000 ghostly tons of supplies. The stacks of supplies were made of plywood

A British Matilda II Infantry tank showing "Sunshield" truck camouflage, with one half on and the other half off. When fully closed up like a clam, the tank looked like an ordinary lorry. This photograph was taken in the Middle East Command Camouflage Development and Training Centre at Helwan, Egypt, 1941.

bed frames, old fuel cans, wicker tomato cases, dummy railway tracks and lots of wire. Over each of the more than 700 heaps were tied down bales of open-mesh cloth, dark-green steel wool and dark garnish nets. Round and round these stacks of "supplies" drove a squad of lorries to add to the impression of activity.

Back at the northern end, an eight by five-mile (thirteen by eight-kilometre) rectangle named "Martello" was staked out as a giant lorry and supply park. Seven hundred Sunshield-enclosed tanks playing the part of lorries, 700 dummy lorries and 4,000 actual lorries pulled in from distant reserves filled the park. In Martello, each parking place for a Sunshield-covered tank had been plotted and numbered on a map for the transition from dummy to covered tank the night before the springing of BERTRAM. In the dark, the tanks rolled up to their designated spot and the Sunshield was clamshelled into place. Seven hundred dummy lorries became tanks, adding to the 700 Sunshielded tanks already in place facing the unsuspecting German spotters. The same ruse was accorded the heavy guns slipping into their "Cannibal" cloaks. The noise of the tanks was covered by a false radio message made available to German listeners concerning a late-night training exercise. British infantry had been dribbled forward during the chilly pre-October nights to huddle in camouflaged trenches. No fires were permitted.

In the south, poorly camouflaged dummy guns set up for the German's benefit as an attempt to inflate the British army's firepower were replaced with real artillery. The 13th Corps in the south dashed forward in several phoney raids. "Sloppy" search-light work illuminated some of the fake "Chinese" infantry who were disembowelled in flurries of cloth and cardboard "guts" by German machine-gun fire. Activity along the southern front increased, giving every impression of an impending future attack.

And still, Rommel's *Fngerspitzengefühl* must have itched like mad, because even as the main British offensive was obviously coming from the south, the northern approach could still be a sideshow. He split his forces, keeping his 15th Panzer and the Italian Littorio Division in the north and sending his 21st Panzer and Ariete Divisions south to Munassib. With his dispositions made, Erwin Rommel made another decision he recorded in his command diary, "C in C – Commander-in-Chief – decides to begin his health cure right now – at once."[8]

His reconnaissance commander, Hans von Luck commented, "He was visibly weak ... and completely worn out ... The tears of a great

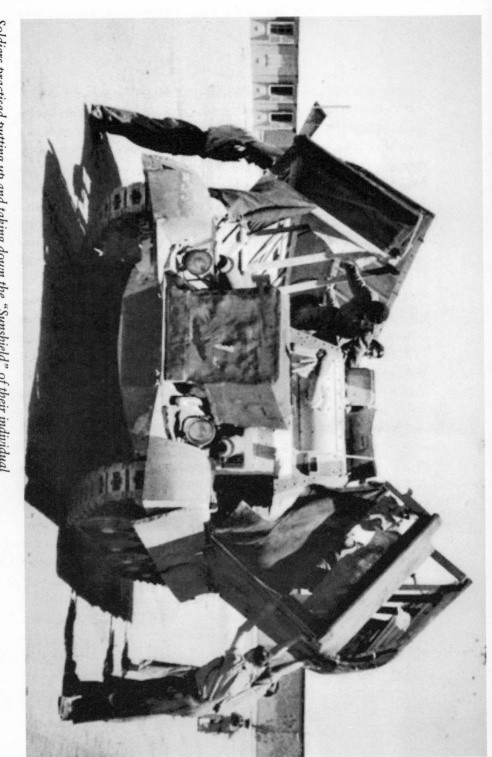

Soldiers practised putting up and taking down the "Sunshield" of their individual tank until they were able to do it quickly, even at night time.

man worn down moved me as much as anything I saw in the war."

Even as Rommel left for Austria, his departure was kept secret from the Allies. His phantom presence on the battlements was worth ten Panzer divisions. The Afrika Korps command was handed over to the aging General Georg Strumme as a stand-in for the absent "Fox". [9]

In the days before Montgomery's offensive launch, fake radio traffic was increased in the south suggesting the movement of heavy units preparing for battle. During the nights, Brigades of the 1st Armoured Division and the entire 10th Armoured Division rolled north into Sunshield position beneath the desert stars.

Back with his "Magic Gang" and dummy manufacturing line, Jasper Maskelyne chafed for a real assignment. He was tired of supervising grunt work and messing about with deception schemes that either were unappreciated or came to naught. His naval misdirection sleight-of-hand projects had shown particular merit. He had bent Barkas' ear at every opportunity and now as BERTRAM was winding down, his stage training cried out for one great illusion all his own.

Maskelyne's work on BERTRAM had not gone without notice and he was called away from his dummy workshop to a meeting of BERTRAM staff. When he arrived at the tent, he found out it was called to celebrate his birthday. Jasper was stunned and sentimentally pleased. He also saw an opportunity to corner Barkas once more. This time, he met with success. For a birthday present, he was assigned to assemble one of his naval deceptions with full support of the Royal Navy at zero hour, 1 a.m. on 23 October. After that announcement and with a plethora of sincere thank-yous, all Barkas saw was Maskelyne's back disappearing out of the tent flap.

On the night of 23 October 1942, a massive British opening artillery barrage fell out of the sky on top of the Afrika Korps' northern lines. Montgomery's gun crews had flung aside the "cannibal" truck covers from their concealed artillery. Following white tapes into the darkness spread out for them by "sappers," infantry with magnetic mine detectors weaved through treacherous mine fields following Matilda tanks fitted with Scorpion chain flails, triggering mines in a wide swath. In the forward lorry park, tank crews tossed off the lorry-shaped "Sunshield" canvas clamshells, scrambled into their Churchills, Grants, and Shermans, gunned the engines to life and rumbled forward as their turrets began searching for Panzer targets.

To add to the Wehrmacht's total confusion, from the southern approaches the guns of the Free French Division commander, M.P. Koenig, ripped loose a heartfelt barrage at Rommel's army, which had humiliated the French in 1940. Above the Nazi positions, Wellington bombers roared in, dropping their bombs on pre-targeted artillery. At the German staff headquarters, dinner had just ended when General Stumme and his companions were jarred by the first volleys of explosions as they walked across their HQ compound. Stumme finished his wine and left his bunker as the explosions let up. He had the "Devil's Garden" for protection – a million land mines – offering a selection of everything from anti-personnel S-mines, to anti-tank mines, to buried 250-pound (550-kg) aerial bombs. But still, he held his Panzers covering the southern approach in reserve to handle predicted threats from that direction.

With Montgomery's attack well underway and the Eighth Army chugging forward through the mine fields, their progress measured in dead and shattered infantry and demolished tanks, Jasper Maskelyne blinked his signal lamp three times. Three swift torpedo boats gunned their engines, as did three barges also parallelling the Mediterranean beaches a short distance from the Fuka Luftwaffe airfield. Each barge lit off smoke canisters, leaving behind a smoke screen obscuring the attack from the sea. After half a mile (800 metres), they doubled back with fresh smoke, making the screen almost opaque as Royal Navy crews pumped deck-gun rounds into the gathering beach defenders.

With their eyes facing north and south, the German battalions were startled when the next sounds of battle erupted *behind* them – from the sea. This sudden assault on German communications lines at Baggush and Fuka airfields sucked Afrika Korps defences away from Montgomery's steamroller attack towards the sounds of British motor torpedo boats (MTBs), crackling explosions, clattering anchor chains and shouted orders from the midst of a huge smoke screen engulfing the Mediterranean shoreline.

On the invading speedboats, phonographs were powered up into large loudspeakers, screaming the sounds of an amphibious invasion. The other barge crews heaved oily smoke pots over the side to mimic the stink of diesel attack craft. A hand-cranked siren wailed. Jasper set off canned artillery "flashes" as the barges' deck guns provided the explosions.

Meanwhile, on shore, frantic calls from German 90th Light Infantry reserves sent to defend against the invasion prompted Luftwaffe bombers and fighters to divert from the Eighth Army's massive attack. Instead, they turned to bomb and strafe this seaborne invasion fleet. Soon, artillery shells began to fall among the smoke-shrouded speedboats and barges, bringing cheers from Jasper Maskelyne and his ragtag crews. As the shells fell closer during the "fleet's" fourth pass down the beach, the crews aboard the slower barges abandoned their craft and crowded onto the speedboats. With the smoke screen abating and the German bombers on the way, Maskelyne's Magic Gang and Royal Navy gunners sped away into the dark. The Nazi shore defenders and the arriving Luftwaffe found only three abandoned barges bobbing in the surf on an empty Mediterranean Sea.[10]

It was during the opening assault that the absent Rommel's designated commander, General Stumme, made a probing sortie in a half-track to the northern lines and blundered into an anti-tank ambush and suffered a fatal heart attack. General Ritter von Thoma took over the reins and began to sort order from the German chaos until he was eventually taken prisoner.

Erwin Rommel cut short his medical leave in Austria and hurried back to North Africa to stem the terrible rout that seemed to be building from this October attack that was supposed to happen on 7 November, at least according to the best German intelligence. Montgomery's initial launch had finally been blunted, but he had sufficient reserves to send out another wave of armour in a broad front and move the guns forward as the infantry continued to press. The British could afford some attrition in their force, while the Wehrmacht's losses of precious Panzers and veteran fighters began to verge on the terminal. Italian support, battle-weary at best, began collapsing as they surrendered, or, following their leaders, fled the battlefield.[11]

Rommel had arrived in time to organize his retrograde manoeuvre. To save lives, the Field Marshal asked Adolf Hitler to permit a full retreat. Hitler refused the request. Seeing his North African mission to control the Suez Canal and stamp out British influence in the oil-rich Middle East ending in a humiliating failure, Hitler made one of his "last man – last bullet" defence rants. Rommel's battlefield reality offered no choice, but to save what remained of his Afrika Korps from total annihilation by the swarming British. He was also pincered by the Americans, whose Operation TORCH had unloaded on the Algiers shore.

The special bond between Hitler and Rommel was fractured by the eventual loss of the North African Campaign. To save some face and help maintain Erwin Rommel's mystique, the former Desert Fox was given command of Hitler's "Atlantic Wall", the fortifications along the Channel Coast that he believed would render France invulnerable to Allied attack.

BERTRAM and TREATMENT were the curtain calls for Dudley Clarke after two years in the field. The British victory at El Alamein had stamped the seal of approval on battlefield deception.

Monty and Rommel would face off again, but this time in company with American troops. At first, dismissed as amateurs who could not fight, the Americans had battled back from a brutal defeat at North Africa's Kasserine Pass on 14–24, February 1943 with a face-saving semi-victory at El Guettar led by a new American commander, George S. Patton Jr. A flamboyant warrior, he was building his own reputation and myth to rival the fame and respect the Desert Fox had built up and in due course he would be competing with Patton for glory when the Allies invaded Hitler's Europe in 1944.

The British summation of the decoy and deception efforts on the outcome of El Alamein was realistically presented by Colonel Geoffrey Barkas, one of its main exponents:

"Though none of us was so foolish as to think that it had been won by conjuring tricks with stick, string and canvas, we could at least feel that we had earned our keep … It was good to feel that camouflage had helped to put the fighting men in battle on more favourable terms, and so to purchase victory at a lower price in blood."

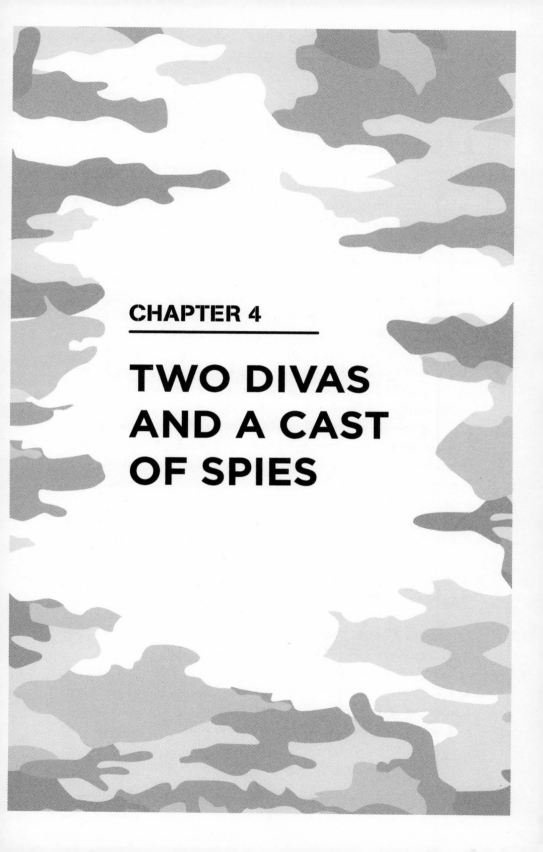

CHAPTER 4

TWO DIVAS AND A CAST OF SPIES

Dossiers and intelligence gathered by the Germans on the 1943 North African campaign revealed two outstanding command- ers: British General Bernard Law Montgomery and American Lieu- tenant-General George S. Patton Jr. Between them, they had beaten their best German counterparts, including Field Marshal Erwin Rommel and the veterans of the vaunted Afrika Korps. However, two more divergent combat styles could not be imagined, let alone teamed up in a common cause. Both were a mixture of born-to- the-colours commanders and creatures of calculated theatrical pos- turing well beyond the leadership requirements for general officers. Each developed his style as they climbed their separate promotion ladders. They also shared some common qualities: to their military colleagues, they were insufferable and egotistic. Both believed in dis- cipline in the ranks and both expressed a visceral love for their men and cast a blind eye to the casualty counts resulting from vigorous and competitive offensive campaigns.

Their troops responded in kind, expressing a pride in their generals, yet sometimes engaging in black humour when the generals indulged their compulsive egos. Montgomery preferred to assemble massive asset inventories before launching any offensive thrust. This slowed his advances and allowed opposing German generals like Rommel to dig in formidable obstacles in depth including minefields and Panzer divisions. When Montgomery's attack finally thundered down on his adversary, the blow was all-enveloping and usually successful. When it was not, the butcher's bill was long and bloody. He was stubborn and willing to spend troops to gain his advantage no matter how hard the slog, as in advance through the German mine fields at El Alamein. Victorious headlines at home were important to Montgomery.

George S. Patton was also a publicity hound. His wealthy family and Virginia Military Institute-West Point background helped create a soldier shaped by the upper crust of command. He was a cavalry trooper with an extensive collection of polo ponies and expertise with the sabre, but also had the skills to lead a squadron of tanks wearing a tanker's uniform he designed himself. In the First World War, he and Douglas MacArthur seemed to vie for stopping a German bullet in the trenches, parading about, urging their commands forward, always forward, shaming the men with their bravado. They both came away virtually unscratched.

Patton's military career was star-crossed due to his eccentricities, ego and distrust of authority. However, once given an order, though he huffed and puffed and raged, he carried it out – which would be demonstrated by his command of his army following their arrival in North Africa.

Montgomery and Patton were high on the Wehrmacht command's list of generals to watch as German intelligence sifted the clues as to the Allies' next strike. These two very dangerous commanders were certain to be involved.

Actually, the Allies had pinpointed Sicily as their next target at the Casablanca Conference in January 1943. The island sat next to the toe of the Italian boot and overlooked the Mediterranean sea-lanes. They called their invasion plan OPERATION HUSKY. Montgomery shared command of the invasion force with Patton, a thinly veiled competitive pairing that would ensure maximum effort from both armies. With logistics, strategies and training in full rehearsal, concern that the plan might become known to the Germans grated on the Allied hierarchy. Churchill later commented, "Anybody but a damned fool would know it was Sicily."

The extent of the preparations was impossible to hide from German spies, but where the invading forces would land and when had to remain unknown – or falsely known. A scenario for a two-point invasion was floated: invade the Greek islands that opened the door to the Balkans *and* attack Sardinia as a direct path to southern France. It was a logical division of command for the two prickly commanding divas, Montgomery and Patton, and it was strategically acceptable. Now, the German High Command and the

Lt. General George S. Patton Jr. commanded the US Third Army in France and Germany following the Allied invasion of Normandy in June 1944. He was aided by the 23rd HQ Troops' deceptions in his relief of Bastogne during the Battle of the Bulge, and Hitler reportedly called him "that crazy cowboy general".

gun-shy Rommel, who had been badly out-foxed in Africa, had to swallow this lie.

MI5 had a group that dealt with double agents – German spies who had been turned to work for the Allies – named the XX Committee, or the Double-Cross Committee. Already adept at intrigue, the Double-Cross Committee took on the job.

In 1940, the Germans had begun feeding agents into Britain to provide information concerning the island's defences and force strength – under the code-name LENA – against Hitler's planned invasion, Operation SEALION. Meanwhile, every British transmitting station was pinpointed for monitoring by the German *Funkabwehr* wireless and cryptanalytic service. MI5's Radio Security Service (RSS) eventually became Section C of MI8 before finally being taken over by MI6 as its Section VIII was charged with intercepting any spy transmissions to or from Mainland Europe.

One day in 1940, a German agent sent a message from Hamburg to a German spy ship in the North Sea. Intercepted, this transmission led to breaking the *Abwehr* agents' hand-sent code (as opposed to the German Enigma machine encoded system that was separately broken by Polish intelligence and the British cryptanalytical station at Bletchley Park). Breaking that manually sent code meant that now the RSS stations could spot a coded message sent to the German spies in Britain and that spy's reply. The location of the code's transceiver was pinpointed, and the spy was scooped up by MI5. Spies who survived the arrest raid were offered the option of becoming double-agents working for the Double-Cross Committee. Virtually all the captured agents accepted. These weary souls who chose to save their skins – Third Reich be damned – reinforced skilled British agents, such as the one code-named GARBO (see Chapter 13) and another called BRUTUS. These two expertly played their parts, masquerading as Nazi sympathizers while creating mythical spy networks that fooled the *Abwehr* right up to the end of the war – and for years after.[12]

MI5 files released 50 years after the end of the war revealed that 70 British spies working for Germany were prosecuted for sending, or carrying war secrets to the FHW (*Fremde Heere West* – the intelligence organization for the OKH *Oberkommando des Heeres*, the German Supreme High Command) or the *Abwehr*. Most had been picked up by MI5 agents posing as *Abwehr* contacts.[13]

The British and Allies took advantage of the intelligence derived from breaking the German Enigma code (ULTRA) and the Japanese (MAGIC) to keep a detailed and updated view of Axis strategies, tactics, troop dispositions, command changes, but most important – for the business of deception – Axis reactions to battlefield illusions.

CHAPTER 5

OPERATION MINCEMEAT

Faced with feeding the German High Command a convincing story for a staging point to the invasion of the Italian mainland – preferably the Greek islands and Sardinia – the Allies needed to create an intelligence windfall for the *Abwehr* which bore no MI5 fingerprints.

After floating some ideas, MI5 officials recalled an incident involving neutral Spain. A British Sunderland flying boat had crashed into the sea off Cadiz and a passenger was washed ashore carrying a letter referring to Operation TORCH, the Allied invasion of French North Africa. The pro-Nazi "neutral" Spanish had returned the letter, but had they read it? In North Africa, Dudley Clarke had made the Afrika Korps a gift of British plans planted in a scout car wreck. This "haversack ruse" might work again. Having roped the Germans into that con once, the *Abwehr* would be extra cautious of a similar "gift".

From this trace of a concept, Flight Lieutenant Charles Cholmondeley, a 25-year RAF officer, conjured up a deception that involved not only the deducible location of the proposed invasion, but a dead body to deliver it. After considerable thrashing about with plans, the somewhat gruesome, but oddly workable idea took shape. A corpse would be dressed as a British courier, planted with top-secret, high-level plans and "killed" in a plane crash at sea off Franco's pro-Nazi Spain. In reality, the body would be dumped off the Spanish coast by a submarine. While the original papers would find their way back to the British, copies must end up in the Nazi's diplomatic pouch for fine-tooth-comb examination by the *Abwehr* intelligence service.

The primary intelligence task would be to make both the courier and his papers seem entirely authentic. Even a faint whiff of fakery would ring bells throughout the German Mediterranean, dissuading the Axis from shifting assets to any place but Greece and Sardinia, and literally drawing a circle around Sicily as the already suspected invasion point. Cholmondeley brought in Flight Lieutenant

Commander RNVR Ewen Montagu to help him bring off the daring operation, which they code-named MINCEMEAT.

First, they needed a body. Not just any body, but one who had either drowned, or had symptoms of fluid in the lungs. The services of Sir Bernard Spilsbury, renowned British pathologist were requested. He explained that people died in plane crashes regularly and the body did not need to show traces of drowning if the crash impact had done its job. He sought out W. Bentley Purchase, coroner for the St Pancras district of London who confirmed Spilsbury's logic and set out to look for a suitable body. In the meantime, as Montagu wrote later,

"There we were, in 1942, surrounded all too often by dead bodies, but none that we could take. We felt like the Ancient Mariner – 'bodies, bodies everywhere, nor anyone to take!' We felt like Pirandello – 'Six officers in search of a corpse' ... At one time, we feared we might have to do a body-snatch – 'do a Burke and Hare' as one of us put it." [14]

Spilsbury, meanwhile, located a body from a London coroner: a Welsh derelict named Glyndwr Michael, aged about 34, born in a Welsh coal-mining community, motherless, and without any other family ties. In a fit of depression, he had crawled into a London warehouse and killed himself with phosphorus-based rat poison – most likely, Battle's Vermin Killer – a particularly toxic, slow-working poison that left no tell-tale signs like arsenic that suffused the hair and nails of the victim. The body in cold storage assumed a new name, (Acting) Major William Martin, Royal Marines. Now the team working on newly christened Operation MINCEMEAT had to create a person. They began assembling Acting Major William Martin's character a step at a time.

The communications critical to the mission were collected in a worn briefcase. None of the correspondence was important enough for an official courier, but the method of delivery demanded the briefcase and Major Martin arrive in Spain as one package. A dog chain was fashioned with clips at either end and handcuffed to Martin's wrist. The premise was lame, but not beyond reason considering the high command ranks of the correspondents.

For his transport to the Spanish setting, a special canister, six feet-six inches (198 cm) long and 22 inches (56 cm) in diameter was cobbled out of 22-gauge steel with the ends fastened with 16 bolts and each fitted with a carrying handle. The canister had a double shell packed with asbestos wool. A box spanner was fastened to the lid.

With the major reclined and packed around with dry ice, the canister would just fit down the submarine's torpedo loading hatch and nestle below deck solidly in the forward torpedo rack. Only the captain, Lieutenant Bill Jewell knew the identity and role of the submarine HMS *Seraph's* canned guest. The winds and tides off Huelva were suitable, if not perfect, but if the Major did not hit his mark on the beach and instead drifted back out to sea on the ebb tide, the operation would flop.

Hedging their bets, Dudley Clarke of "A Force" and John Bevan in London had whipped up a tub-thumping public relations effort called OPERATION BARCLAY for the grand invasion of Greece and Sardinia. Hints of an approaching Greek invasion began showing up at embassy parties in neutral countries. A gathering of dummies: tanks, gliders, landing craft and their assembly facilities emerged in Cyrenaica – just within range of Axis recon aircraft. A squadron of very real RAF fighters was sent aloft at each German plane's appearance to shoo them away. Greek language speakers were recruited and Greek drachmas were being snapped up on the foreign exchange. British troops practised amphibious landings in Egypt, while leaflets were distributed describing "hygiene in the Balkans" with stunning clarity and detail.

On 30 April, less than a mile off the Huelva beach, HMS *Seraph* surfaced after waiting for the local sardine fishing fleet to sail above them a further mile into the bay. The crew lugged the canister up to the foredeck and was dismissed below due to the "top-secret optical instruments" being launched. Lieutenant Jewell at spoke the funeral service, a bit of Psalm 39.

"I will keep my mouth as if it were a bridle: while the ungodly is in my sight. I held my tongue and spake nothing: I kept silence, yea, even from good words; but it was pain and grief to me."

With that, the officers picked up the frail body, eased it into the sea and Major William Martin, Royal Marines, made his entrance.

In his official report of the mission, Lieutenant Jewel chose to write that, after being riddled with gunfire, the canister "was seen to sink". In a postcard sent from Gibraltar to Montagu, Jewell wrote, "Parcel delivered safely." A death notice was published in Britain.

All of the signs that the ruse had worked confirmed Hitler's belief that the Allies were preparing to invade the Balkans through Greece and Sardinia. The High Command began juggling their assets to defend against these obvious invasions, while leaving the highly respected Herman Göring Armoured Division as a token defence on Sicily, where any attack would probably be a feint.

As ULTRA and A-Force codemasters decoded the German build-ups in exactly the wrong places, Montagu received a note: "Mincemeat swallowed whole." The Allies huge accumulation of invasion forces was impossible to hide, but most of the Nazis felt secure in their preparation – except for Doctor Joseph Goebbels, the German propaganda minister, who had reservations about the dead man's gift, its timing, its place of discovery. For the propaganda master and German film-maker, the whole business was just so … "theatrical".

On 10 July 1943, Operation HUSKY dropped on poor Sicily like a thunder clap. The Italian defenders were rolled up. The two landings, one each by Patton and Montgomery, were secured and they raced toward Messina via separate routes. While many thought the divided commands were in competition, Montgomery's Eighth Army was slowed by German resistance. Monty yielded Messina to

Patton, who continued to lunge ahead along a coastal road, while General Omar Bradley battled the battle-hardened Göring Panzers tooth-and-nail across the centre of the island.

Still, as the Allies landed, the Germans continued to believe their intelligence and their Führer's prognostications. A squadron of Luftwaffe bombers took off from Sicily to attack phantom invaders heading into Sardinian shores. Rommel, out-foxed in North Africa, still had a reputation as an invasion-killer and seemed the perfect candidate to halt the Allies' Grecian landings. With a fleet of German *Schnellboots* (fast torpedo boats) and three Panzer divisions plucked from France and the hotly contested Russian Front, he scanned the empty Greek sea in vain.

As Patton and Montgomery flogged their troops toward Messina to block the German's withdrawal to Italy, back in London, cheers went up in the headquarters where MINCEMEAT had been hatched.

Though MINCEMEAT was only a part of the overall BARCLAY deception plan, its dramatic and profound impact was predicted in a telegram sent to Winston Churchill, marking the day the Germans took the bait. "Mincemeat swallowed rod, line and sinker."

Operation HUSKY had an estimated duration of 90 days. The island was conquered in 31 days. The cost was high, but nowhere near the estimated butcher's bill.

A history of deception in World War II pronounced MINCEMEAT: "perhaps the most successful single deception of the entire war." Post-war authors such as Hugh Trevor-Roper went even further, calling it "... the most spectacular single episode in the history of deception."

Ben Macintyre, the author of the definitive work, *Operation Mincemeat,* wrote that, though the military needed hell-for-leather soldiers and cool-headed field commanders, wars are also won by, "... the framers of Operation Mincemeat [who] dreamed up the most unlikely concatenation of events, rendered them believable and sent them off to war, changing reality through lateral thinking and proving that it is possible to win a battle fought in the mind, from behind a desk, and from beyond the grave." [15]

CHAPTER 6

UNTYING THE ITALIAN BOOT: SALERNO & ANZIO

The freshly formed 21st Army Group also needed experienced deceivers for landings in the Central Mediterranean and Middle East. In July 1943, with Sicily being dissected by Monty and Patton, deception planners turned their devious minds to Salerno near Naples, Anzio on the road to Rome and the southern coast of France. The Mediterranean, and specifically, the port of Salerno was now the key front for the deceivers. General Archibald Percival Wavell had had the foresight to bring the eccentric military genius, Dudley Clarke and his small A-Force staff to Cairo in 1940. Since then, his formidable outfit had accumulated a considerable reputation for deception and as a result, key people had been plucked away to London.

Yet Operation BOARDMAN, the deception operation to accompany landings at Salerno, could not be developed out as long as HUSKY was still battling its way through Sicily in the summer of 1943.

To hedge his bets, Eisenhower had ordered General Mark Clark to draft plans for the invasion of Sardinia if Sicily proved unfeasible. Searching farther south brought the planners' attention to the wide sandy beach at Salerno with its elbow room for infantry and manoeuvring tanks. The Americas named their deception invasion AVALANCHE and on 26 July the Combined Chiefs gave official approval for a September assault on the welcoming beaches south of Naples.

Poised across the Sicilian narrows at Messina was Montgomery's XIII British corps. The master plan, called BAYTOWN had Montgomery's Eighth Army crossing the Straits of Messina to land on the toe of the boot unopposed on 3 September. The American landing at Salerno, farther up the shin, was set for 9 September against a supposed defence of six German divisions. Montgomery hated BAYTOWN because it placed him 300 miles (480 kilometres) from Salerno, and supposed an unopposed march covered by the withering firepower of a fleet of Allied battleships, destroyers and air support from offshore aircraft carriers. Mark Clark's plans had him taking Naples within five days of landing. However, Salerno's topography of wide beaches, two dividing rivers and mountainous terrain around the landing zones, which was favourable to determined resistance by German artillery, challenged his optimism.

The only rapidly deployable deception left to American planners was Operation BOARDMAN: false radio intercepts to be picked up by the *Abwehr*. These would suggest the Allies were aiming their post-Sicily attentions at attacking through the Balkans and other far-flung invasion destinations including Sardinia, the Greek Peloponnese and the South Coast of France by direct assault from the United States and by way of the Azores – any beach, in short, that was *not* Salerno. However, the most obvious choice to any half-way sentient military tactician had to be Salerno. The situation was complicated by Italy's surrender. By then Mussolini was in full flight from his supporters, many of them intent on inflicting murderous justice on their former leader. To avoid complete collapse, Hitler ordered 12,000 elite airborne troops and 24,000 men and 150 tanks of the veteran 3rd Panzergrenadier Division to the outskirts of Rome.

Deception Plan BARCLAY was now initiated, featuring bogus attacks on Greece, Sardinia and Southern France with an accompanying script telling the story of Allied reluctance (read "fear") to attack the Italian mainland against those reinforcing German divisions. Allied planners, the BARCLAY messages insisted, had shifted their full attention to Sardinia in late August and from there planned to launch an invasion into Europe.

At this point, Allied planning for the AVALANCHE landings had reached an impasse. The attack on Sardinia suggested by Eisenhower as an alternative to a Salerno blood bath was cancelled and the debate between the Americans and British turned into a shouting match. Finally, on 30 August, only ten days before the British and American invasion forces were to land on their designated Salerno beaches did British General Alexander receive his attack orders.

According to the *Army War College Analysis of World War II (AWC)*, plotting of the tangled deception called Plan BOOTHBY, designed by A-Force to scatter German forces all over Italy's boot was finally put down on paper in mid-August:

"... to prevent any concentration near the landing beaches at Salerno. Plan BOOTHBY, drafted on 14 August *for the landings less than a month away*, covered both Operation BAYTOWN and AVALANCHE; the 'story' sold to the Germans through double agents and other means was that the Allies intended to undertake two and possibly three Operations against the mainland.

"After all, the Allies were aware the Germans expected a landing on the mainland at any time – London and AFHQ had been announcing that for several months before the landings (in a war of nerves with the Italian government.) One of the operations, conducted by XIII Corps, was to be mounted against Crotone in southern Italy from Sicily; the second to be launched against the mainland was to be by British 3rd Corps from the Middle East on September against the heel of Italy. In addition to these operations, the Allies were to assault Sardinia with the British 10th Corps including the use of British 1st Airborne Division from Tripoli, and Corsica would be attacked by two French Divisions and the 82nd (US) Airborne Division, all on 5 September 1943. Directly after the Allies established themselves on Corsica, the US 5th Army and the British 5 Corps were to assault the coast between southern France and northwest Italy but no firm destination had been reached." [16]

A-Force, as was their style, planned an air reconnaissance of the areas concerned, and hit-and-run raids against Crotone. They tried some bi-lingual pamphlet dropping in northern Italy featuring concentrations of Allied troops in greater numbers than were actually taking part in the invasion of Salerno, or British divisions crossing over from Messina. There was the cursory bombing of cover targets in Sardinia and Corsica and the blasting roads behind troops in the south of Italy to discourage their "escaping from the advancing

Allied hordes". To make life even more difficult for the defenders, radio broadcasts in the clear were directed to Italian partisans to vent their humiliation on the Nazi "Crucco" (the disparaging Italian nickname for German soldiers). The Allied high command's ossified planning of their attack on the Italian mainland meant that all these notional diversions had to be quickly thrown together using double agents on their Morse keys and microphones.[17]

The defending Germans, on the other hand, were disciplined and prepared. Field Marshal Albert Kesselring would command the forces opposing Mark Clark's eventual publicity-seeking "capture" of Rome and his subsequent bloody slog up the Italian boot. Clark's four offensives against Kesselring's defensive Gustav Line between January and May 1944 incurred heavy casualties in an attempt to penetrate it. To try and break up Clark's stagnant force, on 22 January the Allies made an amphibious landing in Anzio, further up toward the knee of the boot, in an attempt to outflank the Germans. The landing was one huge successful deception, landing and taking the Germans by complete surprise. Operation SHINGLE was commanded by Major-General John P. Lucas. Instead of quickly advancing to destabilize the formidable Gustav line, Lucas gathered all his forces on the Anzio beachhead which lay in a commodious basin surrounded by a circle of mountains. As he gradually assembled his troops, a GI scouting party set off in a Jeep on an open road from the beach. The party drove to the outskirts of Rome unchallenged. Their return information of the possibility of a clear shot at the Italian capital was discounted by Lucas. End of deception.

The Germans were overjoyed at Lucas's Montgomery-like build-up of Anglo-American assets before attacking. The Germans studded the mountains with artillery facing directly down into the beach and ringed the open basin with machine guns and snipers, mixing German defenders with the formidable Italian SS "Vendetta" Rifle battalions. The Allied invaders had no place to hide. After being enfiladed on the bloody Anzio beachhead and struggling with mounting casualties, Lucas was sent home and General Lucian Truscott took over on 22 February.

Eventually, Truscott enabled a breakout, but instead of messing with the German 10th Army communications where they were holed up in a monastery atop Monte Casino with a 360-degree view of the valley below, Clark commanded Truscott's force to head for Rome and prepare to enter the undefended capital. He would meet them there for the parade into the city. Ordered to finish off a major part of the retreating German 10th Army, General Mark Clark chose to stage "the Conquest of Rome" on 4 June 1944. He led his triumphant troops to accolades and heroic international press coverage and faced only jubilant Italian civilians and the Pope in the undefended "Open City". The German 10th Army remnants escaped to Kesselring's next line of defence, the Gothic Line and their resistance added significantly to the total of 312,000 Allied casualties required to liberate Italy.[18]

As the battle for Salerno moved inland from the beaches, the Germans pulled up stakes in Sardinia and Corsica, likely motivated by notional threats from the Allies in support of the landings in Sicily and Salerno. They were just as likely shortening their communication lines in light of the Allies' latest thrust. In either case, on 12 September Hitler ordered German forces out of Sardinia to Livorno by way of Corsica. Two days later, helped along by U.S. airborne landings, the Allies occupied Sardinia without a shot being fired and followed up by seizing Corsica on 3 October.

With the Germans retrenching their Mediterranean forces onto the European mainland, there were fewer and fewer opportunities to plan and execute additional deception exercises. Dudley Clarke could read a map, and in the late summer of 1943 everything pointed to his A-Force assisting in the strategic planning and execution of OVERLORD, the code-name for the planned Allied invasion across the English Channel. In September 1943, Clarke suggested an organization be formed to support OVERLORD using

British A-Force as a model and co-ordinating deception activities in the Western Mediterranean and Middle East with those directly executed by SHAEF (Supreme Headquarters Allied Expeditionary Force). The Germans would be deceived on a multi-front basis with co-ordinated deceptions and other notional activities across theatres, that would confuse German intelligence units such as the *Abwehr* and OKW (the German armed forces High Command) into verifying them.

The LCS in London, which acted as a policy-making body for the British Chiefs of Staff and as a co-ordinating point with the Americans, was not a military operational level planning and executing group like A-Force. In the autumn of 1943, SHAEF – now in charge of OVERLORD – offered the command of the deception program, BODYGUARD to Dudley Clarke, but he declined and Colonel Noel Wild, Clarke's deputy in Cairo, was appointed instead. Wild arrived in London on Christmas Eve 1943, unaware he was to be head of Eisenhower's deception planning organizations – the post was to be one of the most important jobs for the invasion. A-Force, in contrast, was suffering attrition of other valuable personnel to the planning for Normandy and the landings in southern France, which reflected the shift in emphasis to the western European area.

Much of this raiding stemmed directly from the friendship between President Roosevelt and Winston Churchill. Churchill had a love of deception's drama, the theatrical sleight-of-hand, clever impersonations and then the reveal as the curtain came down. He ran on and on in their conversations in Washington about Operation BERTRAM in North Africa and Montgomery's use of decoys, false wireless transmissions and the creating of an entire faux battlefield: infantry, tanks, half-tracks, artillery and camouflage misdirection.

General Eisenhower wrote of British combat deceptions in *Crusade in Europe*:

"In the early days of the war, particularly when Britain stood alone in 1940 and 1941, the British had little with which to oppose the German except deception. They resorted to every type of subterfuge, including the establishment of a dummy headquarters and the sending of fake messages in order to confuse the German as to the amount of military strength available and, more important than this, its disposition."

CHAPTER 7

FORTITUDE
– WHEELS
WITHIN
WHEELS

In Washington, at the May 1943 TRIDENT Conference, called to co-ordinate Allied strategy for the opening of a new front in France, Lieutenant-General Sir Frederick Morgan was tasked with simultaneous planning of three phases of the cross-Channel invasion to planning group COSSAC at its Norfolk House HQ. Phase One was the actual OVERLORD invasion in 1944, Phase Two was a wishful, uncontested return to the continent in case of a German collapse, while the third phase was "… an elaborate camouflage and deception scheme extending over the whole summer with a view to pinning the enemy in the east and keeping alive the expectation of large-scale cross-Channel Operations in 1943" (Operation COCK-ADE). The desired elements for the invasion included: broad, shallow beaches within striking distance of Allied air power and accommodating sufficient attackers to overwhelm the German defenders. A large port was also necessary to allow shipping for re-supply as the invasion moved inland. The Dieppe Raid and the invasion of North Africa had identified a number of serious problems. Both the landings on Sicily and those on the Italian mainland showed the Allies' idea of amphibious landings still verged on the primitive. On 5 June 1943, Morgan made his presentation and added three subsidiary proposals: STARKEY, WADHAM and TINDALL.

Morgan's staff had concluded that the disastrous Dieppe Raid had suggested to the Germans that they could defend major coastal invasions without the assistance of any mobile reserves. To get the OKW's attention, STARKEY would simulate a huge invasion adding up to the opening of a second front on the beaches between Boulogne and Le Touquet sometime between 8 and 12 September. Thinking ahead, the STARKEY planners figured that, even if intact, the French Channel ports could support no more than nine divisions. An obvious follow-up invasion force was needed.

WADHAM would suggest the sending in of this force in the form of an airborne and seaborne assault on the Brittany peninsula to capture Brest by 30 September once STARKEY had sucked in the

German reserves. TINDALL would contain German reserves in Norway by mounting a thrust in November threatening Stavanger. Capturing Norwegian airfields would allow an invasion force of three divisions to come ashore under air cover. This was aimed to counter any German disbelief that all three operations could be launched in the same month.

The sheer size and complexity of the concentric operations had the conservative military chiefs scratching their heads, but the concept of strategic deception was taking hold, so the green light was lit. They were not the first planners to be nagged by such doubts when faced with the need for a deception of such complexity. Of course, that military Bible, Clausewitz's *On War*, had an opinion.

"To prepare a sham action with sufficient thoroughness to impress an enemy requires considerable expenditure of time and effort, and the costs increase with the scale of the deception. Normally, they will call for more than can be spared and consequently so-called strategic feints rarely have the desired effect. It is dangerous, in fact, to use substantial forces over any length of time merely to create an illusion. There is always the risk that nothing will be gained and that the troops deployed will not be available when they are really needed."[19]

Sadly, for Morgan and prophetically for Clausewitz, this triple-headed hydra of a strategic deception unravelled even as STARKEY began its actual air offensive over the French coast. The one fatal flaw was putting men ashore in three separate invasions, since there were not enough landing craft in all of England. At best, 500 craft could be displayed to Luftwaffe reconnaissance – about one-tenth the number available for the Operation HUSKY campaign in Sicily. Secondly, COSSAC feared a premature uprising of the French resistance around the empty landing beaches. This would result in wholesale Nazi executions of unsupported resistance members who would be needed later when the actual D-Day invasion took place.

STARKEY might also induce the OKW to consider the threats to the Pas-de-Calais and Brittany good reason to stage their Panzers at a convenient mid-point, in Normandy (where the real landings were planned). And finally, the antique forts at Brest and its approaches were formidable enough without heavy artillery or bombing support. Morgan proposed a British battleship – maybe a rather elderly one – could be sent with its nine or ten-inch turrets to reduce the forts by gun action. The Royal Navy scotched that plan. Risking even an obsolete battleship in the confining waters of the Channel – especially in support of an empty deception – was in their view ludicrous. The press headlines alone would be as bad as the morale-dampening results of Dunkirk and Dieppe.

By this time Operations STARKEY, TINDALL and WADHAM had been deflated beyond recognition. Even Morgan threw in the towel rather than continue with diminishing expectations and putting the real operation in jeopardy. On 9 September 1943, STARKEY was allowed to peter out – after the mounting of an armada of empty vessels sent steaming menacingly towards the French coast – rather than collide with the planned landings at Salerno on the same day.

Morgan's complex deception did have a silver lining. The rumours alone stirred up by its background activities had moved it from a deception that reduced ambiguity by concentrating the enemy's attention on a specific wrong alternative, to a deception that increased the Nazis' uncertainty as to the Allies' intentions in general. As a result, the Anglo-American planners had to improve their planning machinery for any major deception. In addition, those in charge of STARKEY "leaked" the sailing of the expedition through the Special Means Group that handled false wireless transmissions, but the risk of this revelation without confirmation of turned German agents and Garbo's network spurred an Allied reaction. The BBC and Reuters had reported an "exercise" had taken place, causing the Germans to believe the invasion had been launched, reconsidered and recalled. Their anxiety increased as to where to deploy their panzers and mobile infantry units.

The deception planning for actual OVERLORD landing devolved on a new set of cover operations, called FORTITUDE. With SHAEF (designated "Ops B") in charge of OVERLORD planning, Operation FORTITUDE was divided into two sections: FORTITUDE NORTH and FORTITUDE SOUTH. NORTH focused on threatening Germany's Scandinavian acquisitions from notional bases of the imitation 4th Army Group in Scotland. FORTITUDE SOUTH was the key plan focused on the cross-Channel invasion of the European continent and Hitler's "Atlantic Wall". STARKEY's mix of planning and execution failures salved with small successes provided lessons for the devisers of FORTITUDE in both the concept and planning for any cross-Channel invasion. The only remaining deception course for FORTITUDE was to concentrate on the Pas-de-Calais as the primary landing target following a feint landing on Normandy to draw off German reserves. All efforts would be directed toward creating that impression.[20]

Key changes had been implemented because of STARKEY, but they were simply words on paper without the machinery for their implementation by Noel Wild, Dudley Clarke's deputy in the A-Force. SHAEF took over planning for FORTITUDE and inherited the Special Means Staff under Major Roger Hesketh. As American combat forces began arriving in Britain in the summer of 1943, Operation FORTITUDE was already in full swing, with BODYGUARD rounding up German agents infiltrated into Britain under the *Abwehr*'s Operation LENA.

As part of the deception strategy, focusing on the Pas-de-Calais invasion plan, thousands of decoy inflatable tanks, artillery pieces and half-tracks were shipped over from the United States, fashioned by United Rubber and Firestone along with six-wheel lorries loaded with battalions of stuffed-cloth soldiers wearing wicker helmets simulating garrison infantry and jeep "passengers". These FORTITUDE decoys were also available to be added to tactical deceptions once the Allies began to move inland from the invasion beaches. [21]

One of many inflatable dummy 3-ton open-bed trucks used in Operation FORTITUDE to fool the Germans into believing an invasion build-up was occurring at Pas-de-Calais. To aid the deception, inflatable drivers were sometimes placed in the drivers' seats.

Fake Spitfire fighters and airfields were added to fake oil refineries, while imitation bomb and ammunition dumps appeared in empty fields throughout the country. All these pre-invasion physical deceptions were meant to deceive high-altitude German aerial reconnaissance.

To the Americans, most British stagecraft looked crude. Were the Germans that gullible? In fact, the British had learned that the aerial reconnaissance continually carried out by the Germans was not as thorough as that performed by the expert photo interpreters at RAF

Medmenham. After a long period of experimentation beginning in World War I, ultra-sharp stereo cameras had been developed that produced photos viewed through a pair of stereopticon lenses. Ground objects now had three-dimensions photographed in multiple passes by Spitfires, Blenheims and superfast Mosquito fighter-bombers. The German Luftwaffe also had specialized recon aircraft, but the cameras, while they produced sharp pictures with their Zeiss lenses, made photos that were viewed as flat images. Fake shadows painted on the ground could fool a German photo interpreter. Yes, optically, the Nazis were that blind. [22]

Noel Wild directed FORTITUDE SOUTH, with 21st Army Group under the command of General Bernard Law Montgomery responsible for implementing the cover operations. His deception section was headed by Colonel David Strangeways. This officer had distinguished himself in North Africa and had impressed Montgomery with his intelligence, quiet courage and brisk, no-nonsense manner. Strangeways also matched Montgomery in arrogance and his style was the exact opposite of Noel Wild, who was a more typically straight-laced public-school "old boy".

Strangeways literally ripped up Wild's initial FORTITUDE plan at a meeting of SHAEF and LCS and later presented his own rewrite. This new scheme divided FORTITUDE into two parts: pre-D-Day deceptions that would point to Pas-de-Calais as the main invasion front, with the Normandy landings portrayed as a feint to draw off the OKW panzers and heavy infantry. In part two, Strangeways continued the deception, following the Normandy "feint" with a menacing second, larger and deadlier invasion threat designed to further pin Hitler's army groups in place at Pas-de-Calais for days – and maybe a week – to allow the Normandy invasion to develop and break out from the beachhead.

This re-write required the creation of a second, notional army group poised opposite the Pas-de-Calais: troops, armour, fueling, housing and training facilities had to be "created", led by a believable commander, and furnished with a fleet of cross-Channel naval units and landing craft. Of course, this plan would severely tax the number of divisions currently assembling, splitting off actual fighting troops to be part of a decoy force, while making already scarce landing craft and fighting naval units unavailable for the real invasion force.

Strangeways compromised to get the ball rolling; prominent physical deception decoys would be limited to a collection of faux landing craft moored along the south-east coast. All other physical preparations for the Pas-de-Calais invasion would follow the model that had been successful in North Africa's Operation BERTRAM. Troop and vehicular traffic would be simulated through routine radio scripts that would be picked up by the Germans. Reconnaissance flights by the Luftwaffe were few enough over sectors heavily patrolled by the RAF, and densely equipped with anti-aircraft defences. Limited to high altitude runs, the inadequate information in the Germans' flat, non-stereo images worked in the Allies' favour.

This threatening phantom army group opposite the Pas-de-Calais had already been hinted at in earlier bogus radio transmissions, so its name, the First United States Army Group (FUSAG), would not be unfamiliar to Axis operatives intercepting them. Updated information fed to the Germans now confirmed that SHAEF consisted of the 21st Army Group and FUSAG, combining the First Canadian Army (II Canadian Corps and VIII United States Corps) and the United States Third Army (XX Corps and XII Corps), all supported by the U.S. Ninth Air Force.

None of this firepower was directly hinted to the OKW as being aimed at the Pas-de-Calais. However, the indications carefully planted in transmission suggested that this hovering monster, FUSAG, would be launched once the 21st Army Group had landed their lesser, feint attack on the Normandy beaches.

To manage this complex deception, Strangeways produced Plan QUICKSILVER, made up of six parts:

Operation OVERLORD saw the successful invasion of German-occupied Western Europe, beginning with the D-Day landings on 6 June 1944. This photograph, taken a few days later, shows landing ships bringing cargo ashore on Omaha Beach at low tide. In the sky are barrage balloons, which served as obstacles to low-flying enemy aircraft.

Quicksilver I was the basic "story" for Fortitude: the First United States Army Group, (FUSAG) based in the south-east of England, was to land in Pas-de-Calais after German reserves were committed to Normandy.[23]

Quicksilver II was the radio deception part of Quicksilver, involving the apparent movement of units from their true locations to south-eastern England.

Quicksilver III was the display of dummy landing craft, including associated simulated wireless traffic and signing of roads and special areas. The landing craft would be built from wood and canvas and nicknamed "Bigbobs".

Quicksilver IV was the air plan for Quicksilver, including the bombing of the Pas-de-Calais beach area and tactical railway bombing immediately before D-Day.

Quicksilver V was increased activity around Dover (giving an impression of extra tunnelling and additional wireless stations) to suggest embarkation preparations.

Quicksilver VI was night lighting to simulate activity at night where dummy landing craft were situated.

The most important part of Quicksilver was the bogus radio traffic to simulate movements of corps, divisions and battalions of men, armour and air support. The rest dealt with the physical manifestation of this phantom army. Unknown at the time was Germany's slackened interest in radio and aerial reconnaissance. Aerial surveys accomplished at great risk in the face of RAF patrols and ack-ack batteries were challenging enough for the Luftwaffe, and the sheer volume of housekeeping and routine traffic control transmissions produced by the QUICKSILVER units was quite overwhelming. Still, the energy put into constructing FUSAG and broadcasting its importance did not go unnoticed by the *Abwehr*.

One part of QUICKSILVER in particular caught Hitler's eye: the feverish construction of landing craft and their mooring in ports in south-east England, ready to transport FUSAG across the Strait of

Dover to crash against his waiting Atlantic Wall. Hitler was not a navy man, but he understood the value of amphibious landing craft. It was his inability to gather enough of them for his Operation Sea Lion invasion of England – plus the fact that he lacked air superiority – that had put him in the pickle he was in now.[24]

CHAPTER 8

WHENEVER THE TWAIN SHALL MEET

From 1941 to early 1944, the Americans and the British diverged considerably in their styles of conducting the war. The British, with a two-year advantage in experience but limited resources were forced to play the long game, meting out their offensive engagements selectively and devoting much thought to defending Britain itself. The Americans, with bottomless resources, untouched by threat of invasion, managed two wars from two coasts with a fully mobilized industrial and military complex fuelled by vast gold reserves, and a patriotic work force which supplied endless battalions, regiments, divisions, corps and armies of fighting men. The British bided their time in preparation until ready. The Americans went straight ahead, feeding their overwhelming resources into the battles.

This was the fundamental difference between the two nations and their respective, international allies when they came together in 1942 to make war with the German-Japanese-Italian Axis. When America joined the war, the British were already engaged in preparations for the next grand deception, the cross-Channel invasion of Hitler's Third Reich.

In spite of its resources, the American Army's strength just prior to the Japanese attack on Pearl Harbor in December 1941 – including their Army Air Corps – was 130,000, with not enough tanks to cobble together a division. Of the 1,175 planes they could scramble, most were obsolete. As 1942 found the Americans being pounded by the Japanese in the Pacific, and even though President Franklin Roosevelt had instituted a pre-war draft to pull in conscripts to the army, funding to become the free world's arsenal, war production and recruitment centre were just cranking up. Roosevelt welcomed Winston Churchill who had already led Britain through two years of war with Nazi Germany. The Prime Minister was equally delighted to have America as an ally.

In his book, *The Grand Alliance*, Churchill wrote, "No American will think it wrong of me if I proclaim that to have the United States at our side was to me my greatest joy...I thought of a remark which

Edward Grey had made to me more than thirty years before – that 'the United States is like a gigantic boiler. Once the fire is lighted under it there is no limit to the power it can generate'. Being saturated and satiated with emotion and sensation, I went to bed and slept the sleep of the saved and thankful." [25]

But years of post-World War I neutrality, the Great Depression and underfunding of the military had American soldiers training with stove-pipe mortars, wooden guns, lorries with "tank" chalked on the side and aircraft that were gun fodder for the Nazi Messerschmitt and Japanese Zero fighters. Like their colonial cousins during the American Revolution, it was the Yanks' turn to learn guile and deception to counter a superior force, this time as squadrons of panzer tanks and overwhelming air fleets.

In that dark year of 1941, Lord Louis Mountbatten, who had been experimenting with stealthy commando forces using sonic deception to create the false impression of beach landings by large forces, invited a Hollywood movie star to join his Combined Operations Command. Douglas Fairbanks Jr, a member of the American Naval Reserve had been appointed by President Roosevelt to observe (read "spy upon") British naval operations and tactics. His swashbuckling film roles (*Gunga Din, The Corsican Brothers*) and Hollywood star power helped him connect with many of the highest-ranking officers and politicians. He struck up a friendship with Mountbatten.

The Combined Operations Command recorded the sounds of an invasion on turntable records: real troops, real tanks, real landing craft, anchor chains and engines turning over. In brief raids, hidden behind smoke screens, fast motorboats and British MTBs toting these loudspeakers broadcast this "British landing" to on-shore German defenders, while an actual commando harassing force landed unopposed further along the coast. Fairbanks was dazzled by the possibilities such a technique offered an American Navy that was struggling to ramp up its offensive capabilities while feverishly recruiting and building the weapons of war.

Working out of a "haunted" castle at Achnacarry near Loch Arkaig in the Highlands of Scotland, the sonic warriors trained at a secret base near Ballantrae on the coast opposite Northern Ireland. Fairbanks loved the dashing intrigue of roaring across the choppy water, sliding with silent stealth into a pre-dawn target beach and ginning up their sonic landing force to startle Scottish fishermen. Two situations cut short these exhilarating tests. Mountbatten discovered Fairbanks' celebrity was endangering the secrecy of the commandos' work and Fairbanks was anxious to return to the United States with his first-hand knowledge of British deception tactics.

On arriving back in the States, Fairbanks presented a complete, Top-Secret, three-part script for integrating deceptive warfare into the American Navy. First, a section should be created, reporting to the Joint Chiefs of Staff (JCS), which would immediately draft a plan designed to deceive, confuse and mislead the enemy as to the military's actual intentions. Next, an agency should be designated to co-ordinate with the British LCS (London Controlling Section) which oversaw virtually everything involving invasion cover operations, from monitoring radio misinformation to controlling double agents via the Special Means Group. Lastly, his plan asked for an elite amphibious combat unit to be formed to use these developed deceptions in future landings. This plan was dropped in the Navy's lap as the preparations for Operation TORCH – the American amphibious invasion of North Africa in November 1942 – were being finalized. Admiral Ernest J. King was in no mood for movie star theatrics when his own invasion operation was riddled with security leaks by loose-lipped officer personnel.

The Americans were learning the hard way that intense security was absolutely necessary for effective battlefield deception practices. Operation TORCH was in jeopardy of being cancelled. Landing on three North African beaches and convincing the Vichy (Axis-aligned) French not to resist the invasion of the French territories was tricky enough without compromising the operation's security. A new list of Top-Secret, eyes-only recipients was drawn up. Fairbanks didn't make the cut, being only a lieutenant and not a graduate of the elite Annapolis naval academy.

Disappointed, Douglas Fairbanks Jr later wrote, "... King thought the idea just another set of wasteful silly tricks." Much, much later Fairbanks would discover his template for combat deception had been pushed forward for implementation to General Eisenhower's SHAEF and a complete hierarchy of implementers attached to General Omar Bradley's 12th Army Group. Unknown to him, his plan had been taken up, but entrusted to quite different hands to put into practice.

As 1942 dawned, American imaginations and ingenuity were already bridging the deception gap with the British. Some of the best and brightest scientific minds were recruited. The National Research Defense Committee (NRDC) was set up to bring together universities, laboratories and independent scientists to explore fields of science that might benefit the war effort. In February 1942, the Stevens Institute of Technology in Hoboken, New Jersey, was the first to study the concept of sonic deception. Given the project number "17" by the NRDC, experts in the field of sound reproduction and acoustics gathered to determine if sonic deception was feasible. Two of these scientists were Hallowell Davis, a professor of physiology at Harvard Medical School, and Harold Burris-Meyer, responsible for the theatrical stereo system for the Walt Disney film, "Fantasia". An experimental test station for sonic deception was established at an army coastal artillery testing facility in Fort Hancock at Sandy Hook, New Jersey.

In a Top-Secret letter issued on 5 March 1943, Admiral King ordered the Vice Chief of Naval Operations to put out a call for 180 officers and 300 enlisted men to join the "Beach Jumper" programme – Fairbanks' original name for his proposed commando-style unit. These "Jumpers" would simulate landings on enemy shores far away from actual landings.

Fairbanks began canvassing technical schools and universities, even posting at the Notre Dame Midshipman's School an irresistible broadside looking for: "... volunteers for prolonged, hazardous, distant duty for a secret project." The response at each academic institution was overwhelming and soon a "Beach Jumpers" training base was established at Camp Bradford, Virginia. For staging mock invasions of the North Carolina Outer Banks, the Jumpers were allotted six 63-foot (19-metre) Air-sea Rescue Boats, each manned by a crew of six: skipper, first mate, boatswain, two engineers and one anti-aircraft gunner. Fairbanks drove his volunteers with the same force of energy shown by Mountbatten who demanded, "... The problems of these Operations should be handled with an ephemeral combination of force, subtlety, shrewdness, guile and knowledge born of actual experience."

A Hollywood special effects expert, Fletcher Stephens, gave the Beach Jumpers a lesson in creating flash devices to simulate the discharge of medium field artillery, and the use of lightweight pack-howitzers which were dropped with both live paratroops and dummy paratroops which Fairbanks helped design. Dropping with the 102nd and 82nd Airborne in the dark before the dawn landings, these "*gummipuppen*" ("dolls") caused German patrols to blaze away at the dummies that were stuck in the ground with an iron spike and which answered gunfire with triggered firecrackers, smoke grenades and flares. The Americans called their paradummies, "Oscars," while the British SAS tagged them "Ruperts".

On the night of 27 October 1942, just as Montgomery's Eighth Army was in its fifth day of the El Alamein offensive in North Africa, an American war game invasion fleet rode the chop off New Jersey's Sandy Hook Island, ready to "storm" sandbagged positions shielding 300 infantry troops defending the Coast Guard artillery batteries. Above the invasion fleet, a squadron of six aircraft orbited. Three waited for their cue to dive down and lay a dense mist offshore, parallel to the beach. The other three were "armed" with

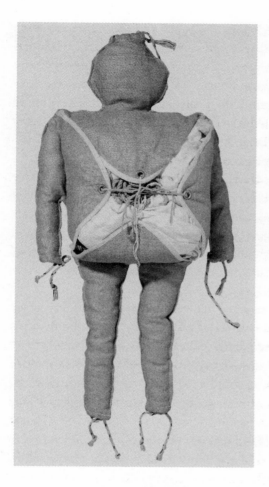

Five hundred "Ruperts" were dropped over France on D-Day to confound the Germans and draw their attention and fire power away from the actual invasion. These half-size "paradummies" exploded with the sound of popping "rifle fire" as they fell, then burst into flames on landing so that the Germans couldn't find them.

flares to illuminate the defenders for the attackers. The invading fleet consisted of a Coast Guard cutter, two converted Gloucester fishing boats and six landing craft. Bobbing nearby, loaded with VIPs and military observers was the yacht, *Dixonia*, loaned to the Army Transport Service by the Walgreen family of pharmacy fame. This invasion manouevre was designed – it was hoped – to confuse the defenders as to the actual landing point and to see, first-hand, the effectiveness of sonic and illumination deceptions.

On cue, the planes dived along the beach and the audio engineers cranked up their huge 500-watt, Western Electric speakers aboard the fishing boats. Large ship-engines roared to life, guttural vrooms of motorboats churned white horses as flares cast their dazzling and eerie glow into the concealing mist of "oil-fog". The sounds rumbled and raced toward the south end of the beach, landing craft hulls slammed down on the chop as shouted loudhailer commands managed the onrushing phantom invaders.

Originally, the sounds were played from portable phonograph records, but jarring, even on a relatively stable boat, caused the needle to pop out of the groove. These phonographs were given the code-name, "water heaters" and they were started with the command, "Heat 'em up!" The name Heaters stuck, but it came to be attached to the entire playback-speaker system – especially the loudspeaker matrix.

The offshore wind continued to tear away the oil-fog smoke screen, forcing the planes to circle back and lay fresh clouds. The defenders "saw" with their ears, believed the small armada had crossed the sand bar and now drove on the *south beach* shoreline. As the troops double-timed southward down the strand, rifles at port arms, the crescendo of arriving landing craft approached just behind the smoke screen.

Meanwhile, five actual landing craft drove up on the *north beach* sand and 300 attacking soldiers flooded onto Sandy Hook, New Jersey – unopposed and victorious.

The Sandy Hook amphibious manouevres convinced all the right people. Satisfied, Douglas Fairbanks Jr went back to Camp Bradford to recruit and train more Beach Jumpers, while the technical staff set to their tasks of developing the field equipment, training engineers and operators to run it, and thinking out strategies for its tactical use.[26]

The invasion of Sicily offered an opportunity to field-test theory into the reality of combat. The planners of Operation HUSKY decided a deception was needed off Cape San Marco, 100 miles

(160 kilometres) west of the HUSKY landing beaches. On the small Mediterranean island of Pantelleria off the coast of Tunisia, which had been recently seized by the U.S. for its small airfield, the Beach Jumpers set up shop and loaded their sonic deception and pyrotechnic gadgetry.

Swivel-mounted speakers in their "Heater" enclosures were mounted amidships in each Air-sea Rescue Boat (ARB). Huge Ohnen electric generators took up the well deck and a beefed-up Bell Labs wire recorder loaded with amphibious landing sounds occupied the port-side deck, while its amplifier sat on the starboard rail between a box of floating time-delay explosives and a rack of smoke pots. Two pairs of .50 calibre machine guns faced out from port and starboard dual mounts flanking the bridge, and a pair of 3.5-inch rockets in their launch racks occupied the bow. Thus armed, on 11 July 1943, the Beach Jumpers in their ARBs finally went to war.

Joining the small armada of four sonic and smoke-armed ARBs and a few Motor Torpedo Boats (MTBs) was U.S. Navy *PT-213* to add firepower support. This first run down the San Marco coast with rocket and smoke pots drew the attention of harassing searchlights and gunfire. On returning, the Jumpers were ordered to carry out a second and much larger-scale operation to really cement German attention to the beaches well west of the invasion sites.

Twenty-four hours later, the deception force left Pantelleria's Scauri Harbor at 20 knots (37 km/h) in two groups. ABLE group consisted of six ARBs and four PT Boats. CHARLIE group encompassed five ARBs, four PT Boats and the destroyer *Endicot* to cover both groups. Their target diversion beaches were off Cape Granitola and Mazara del Vallo. At 9.30 pm, the faux invasion fleet arrived and began setting up their pyrotechnics.

With throttles half-cracked to eight knots (15 km/h), the ARBs closed on the beach, firing rockets and heaving out smoke pots, chugging parallel to the blacked-out shore, laying down a thick smoke screen. Behind this, the "heaters" blared out their ominous chorus of amphibious battle sounds. Pyrotechnic devices flared and rocket barrages exploded. Once again, German searchlights stabbed out into the impenetrable smoke. This time, the PT Boats' heavy return fire did not slack off. A second and third run behind the obscuring smoke produced more blind firing and searchlights from shore. With the screen abating, CHARLIE re-grouped and turned to disappear back into the dark sea.

They were replaced by Group ABLE, whose arrival was greeted by shot and shell. Their commander, Lieutenant Commander Barnes noted in his after-action report:

"The shore batteries by this time were completely alerted. Apparently, the enemy was convinced that a landing was about to take place when it detected large numbers of boats constituting our second group approaching the beach, for they opened up with heavy, accurate, radar-controlled fire before our demonstration could begin. Course was immediately reversed and the range opened. Salvos of six-inch and smaller guns were observed. One shell damaged the rudder of ARB 68 and another fell ten yards astern of a PT. It was considered that the Operation had been accomplished and we withdrew ..."

Facing the fall of heavy shells seeking targets lit up by radar, ABLE's contribution was not needed to attract their audience's concentrated interest. The deception fleet reversed course and withdrew: the ARBs back to Pantelleria and the PT Boats to Bizerte.

A German news broadcast on 13 July announced the repelling of an invasion attempt between Sciacca and Mazara. Captured documents and prisoner interrogations later confirmed the Germans had been completely mystified as to both the scale and date of the HUSKY landings. More important for the Beach Jumpers' sonic and pyrotechnic deception debut, the commanders of the German reserve Panzer force had been uncertain where to commit their counter-attack due to the many landing possibilities.

The finale for the Beach Jumpers in the Mediterranean occurred during the invasion of Southern France (Operation ANVIL-DRAGOON) on 15 August 1944. The simulation of a landing 100 miles (160 kilometres) west of the actual site on the French coast was designed to keep German units pinned down expecting an invasion up through the Balkans.

Lieutenant Commander Fairbanks Jr constructed a Beach Jumper diversion comprised of two groups, East and West, with Fairbanks commanding the Eastern section – the destroyer, *Endicott*, four ARBs, four PTs and the gunboat, *Scarab* (with Fairbanks aboard the gunboat *Aphis*). A full complement of sonic, smoke, rocket and light firepower was reinforced with radar jamming devices. Small boats trailed RCM balloons and box kites as radar targets simulating larger vessels. Aircraft prepared to drop foil fragments ("window") to simulate a fleet of aircraft on German radar. In addition, a full script of false radio broadcast communications would be aimed at German monitors.

On D-1, 14 August 1944, the groups were moving into position when two German corvettes sailed into the deception force and began attacking one of the ARBs. Fairbanks ordered his outgunned group to support the endangered ARB and attacked the two corvettes. With the *Endicot* still coming up, *Aphis* and the *Scarab* closed with the Germans. Exchange of gunfire knocked out the *Aphis'* electronic gunsights. The two aged gunboats continued to slug it out with the two Germans until the *Endicott* arrived and their combined firepower sent the German warships to the bottom. Two hundred and seventy-two German survivors were rescued.

In the meantime, the remains of the Eastern Group and the entire Western Group put up convincing demonstrations of an invasion armada amid heavy German defensive fire. Ultimately, these deceptions confused the Germans enough that the main landing was met with only a mediocre, ineffective defensive force. The engagement marked the closing curtain for the Beach Jumpers in the Mediterranean Theatre. [27]

The tactics were not abandoned, however. The adaptation of British-pioneered sonic deception to naval and land combat applications became an integral part of American strategy for the OVERLORD invasion of Normandy on D-Day in 1944. More actors, artists, sound engineers, architects, and other creative types were skimmed from army ranks to disappear into the Top-Secret world of post-D-Day tactical deception.

The wartime record of Lieutenant Commander Douglas E. Fairbanks Jr, USNR, earned him an impressive row of combat awards. For planning the diversion-deception operations and his part in Operation ANVIL-DRAGOON, he was honoured with the United States Navy's Legion of Merit with bronze V (for valour), the Italian War Cross for Military Valour, the French *Légion d'honneur*, the *Croix de guerre* with palm, and the British Distinguished Service Cross. Fairbanks was also awarded the Silver Star for valour displayed while serving on PT boats in 1942 and was made an Officer of the National Order of the Southern Cross, conferred by the Brazilian government. [28]

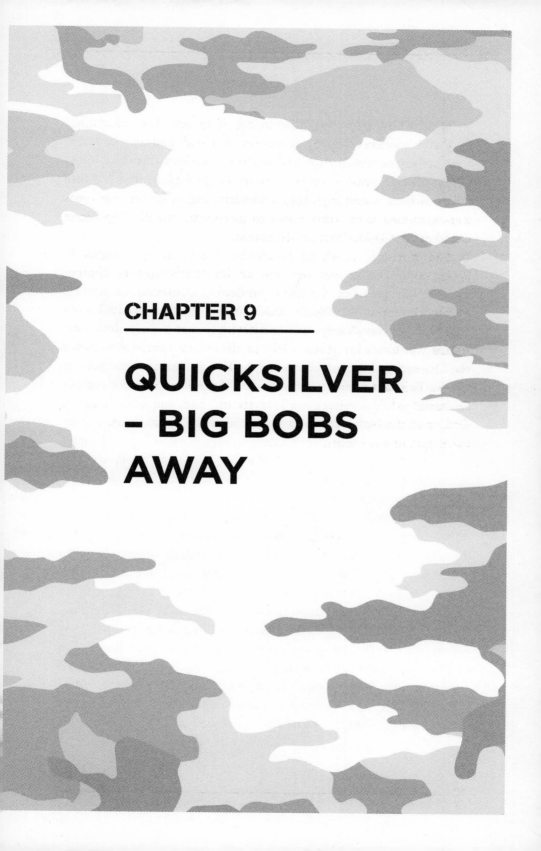

CHAPTER 9

QUICKSILVER – BIG BOBS AWAY

QUICKSILVER was conceived back in the dark months of 1940 when the British faced an indomitable enemy of enormous military strength possessed of a momentum that was crushing Allies across the European continent. Britain stood virtually alone against Adolf Hitler's Germany and knew that every weapon that came to hand must be forged and brought to the breach. The desperate British War Cabinet reached back into their history and settled on deception.

Sir John Turner was Director of Works at the Air Ministry. His knowledge as a qualified pilot and supervisor of air-field construction and infrastructure made him a good candidate for the role of masterminding the creation of decoy sites when it arose. His unit was known as Colonel Turner's Department located in Surrey at the Sound City Film Studios in Shepperton. British weather dictated that most film productions had to be shot indoors; using creatively lit mock-ups to simulate outdoor scenes. Experienced at creating deceptions, these film crews were set to work mocking up dummy aircraft and equipment, besides supervising local builders, farmers and labourers to set up and man the sites. To equip his crews with the necessary skills, Turner also ran a two-week course in deception tradecraft at Shepperton.

The deception also involved the construction of entire dummy towns, known as "Starfish Sites" which were set up as enticing targets for Luftwaffe bombers. They were carefully situated between one and eight miles (1.5 to 13 kilometres) from the real towns, which ought to have been the German bombers' destinations. In broad daylight, these phantom conurbations were clearly nothing more than glorified hen-houses, but when illuminated at night, they could be made to seem like buildings set on fire by incendiaries – an impression that could be made to last for hours. Lighting was added to the Starfish Sites, so that they could be made to resemble whole factories, shipyards or steelworks, and extra touches such as red and green railway signals created the impression of a whole transport

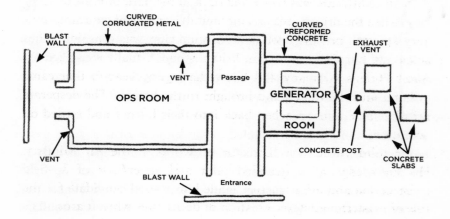

Layout of a typical Decoy Airfield bunker drawn by Doug Willies in 1996.

network. Fine detailing made parts of the Starfish Site appear as if there were open skylights or windows, where a careless worker had failed to comply with blackout regulations.

The decoy operation was on a large-scale, with 630 sites in total, of which 400 were decoy towns or industrial sites, and 230 fake airfields. After the end of the war, it turned out that there had been 443 bombing raids on decoy airfields, more, in fact than against real operation airfields (which were attacked 434 times). The decoy towns were subjected to around 100 Luftwaffe bombing raids, and were hit by around a twentieth of the bomb load, which had been intended for real urban centres. Official calculations indicated that the deception had prevented 2,500 deaths and 3,000 injuries (as against the four civilians who died during air attacks on the decoy sites). If "near-misses" which fell within a few miles of the decoy sites had been included (which official figures did not), then the death toll the deception operation averted would have been even higher.[29]

These successful deception measures during the Battle of Britain inspired General Wavell during the African Desert campaigns. In 1941–42, Brigadier Dudley Clarke's famous A-Force and the inflatable tanks and guns – called "bagpipes" – had befuddled the Germans. The Allied Chiefs of Staff held a meeting in a conference room on a rain-lashed January morning in 1943 to call off Operation ROUNDUP (the predecessor plan of OVERLORD, which called for an invasion of Europe scheduled in the summer of that year). As a stop-gap measure, they decided that deception concepts already in the pipeline would go forward.

A couple of days later at a meeting of ROUNDUP Sub-Committee 3, Sir John Turner was asked, along with the Army Camouflage Development and Training School at Farnham Castle, to examine the possibility of building dummy landing craft that would serve to divert the enemy from actual Allied military deployments. Colonel John Bevan took on what became known as the Special Devices Branch based in London's Cadogan Square. This group of Royal Engineers eventually became famous for fiendishly clever and effective mobile armour and weapons that were important assets ("Hobart's Funnies") on and after D-Day.

The dummy landing craft, with its shallow hull, needed to move easily in estuaries and coastal waters. Not only that, but it must possess enough strength to sustain Force 4 – 13 to 18 knots (24 to 33 km/h) – considered a moderate breeze on the Beaufort scale. Last but not least, the dummies should be quick and easy to assemble in eight hours.

Shortly after the ROUNDUP meeting, Howard Wilton, the managing director of the Cox & Company engineering works near Watford, received an unusual phone call asking his company for co-operation in a highly secret war project. Wilton and his chief design engineer, Chris Toon were invited to Cadogan Square and subsequent meetings with Captain Johnson Marshall in charge of approving design matters.

Toon set to work creating a dummy landing craft, its hull made of a steel tubing frame floating on steel drums. The dummy vessel would resemble a Landing Craft Tank (LCT) Mk-4 with a 31-foot beam, 175-foot length with a 400-ton displacement. Welded three-quarter-inch (1.9-cm) steel tubing fabrications formed the ship's sides, which floated on the sealed metal drums, with canvas covering the framework. Essentially, the dummy was an articulated raft, permitting rapid assembly using fish plates and split pins to produce a bridge-girder construction not unlike the Warren Girder used in designing the Hawker Hurricane fighter plane. The funnel, deck housing and bow doors were pre-made; all parts exactly matching those of the real LCTs and designed to be transported in three-ton lorries for assembly at the final site.

After workers completed the prototype – in a blister hangar at the Cox factory car park – it was taken to the Frensham Great Pond nearby and passed its flotation test with flying colours.

Not long after, on an early spring day in 1943, a small van filled with large wood slabs, hammers, spikes, tarpaulins and other construction gear, lumbered over winding roads through wooded areas and finally pulled up to a narrow beach near Lepe on the Hampshire coast. Its occupants opened the doors, stood up and stretched their legs, breathing in the salt air.

Then they walked along the sand and brush until they found a surface with the right sloping angle good for launching a craft – which they had yet to build. But first they needed simple furniture, benches and tables. Jim Clay, a master builder and leader of the crew supervised construction of the necessary pieces, after which he scurried up a pine tree to which he nailed a simple sign: "Cox's Holiday Camp".

The word "holiday" was a misnomer. For the next several months, this "Robinson Crusoe" camp overlooked the Solent, the 20-mile- (32-kilometre) long, 2 ½ to 5 mile- (4 to 8 kilometre-) wide strait that separates the Isle of Wight from the English mainland. It serves as a major shipping lane for passenger, freight and military vessels. The Solent is also known as the place where the Royal Navy is traditionally reviewed by the monarch of the day. This hallowed ground would serve as a test site for the British Navy's part of Operation QUICKSILVER, a deception concept in which groups of dummy landing craft would be positioned at fake sites away from the actual D-day deployments set for Normandy.

Once the site was ready, with tents, tables, benches and official camp sign, Clay returned to the factory, and gathered a 20-man task force under the direction of Major E. H. Wilton, 20th Battalion, Middlesex Home Guard. He also commandeered a line of lorries and trailers carrying material for the dummy craft. It was time to assemble the prototype parts and put their prop to the acid test. Would it pass its trials at sea?

For security reasons, only the flotation main frame was assembled on the sealed barrels, in just a few hours during low tide. That was the good news. The bad news: when the tide came in, the heavy steel frame sank slowly into the now wet, mushy sand. The workers, up to their waists in water, tried to hoist, push and shove, but their prop stubbornly sat there.

As luck would have it a band of soldiers was double-timing down the beach and offered to help. They managed to loosen the unwelded frame and get it floating to accompanying lusty cheers. But the craft had a mind of its own and, once freed, made its way out into the choppy Solent with a nine-man work party stranded aboard, dressed only in swimming trunks, clinging to the sea-washed framework. The Navy eventually came to the rescue and, using a small tug, towed the craft back to shore. The shivering men aboard were taken to hospital to be treated for exposure.

Now it was time for the sea trials, and to test the effect wave motion would have on their craft. Again, after a small mishap with the naval tug that had been towing it, the device passed this second stage, much to the relief of Chris Toon and John English, the field officer for the trials.[30]

The experiment had succeeded, and the Admiralty, after expressing doubts as to the wisdom of the operation, finally gave its cautious approval. A production site was established in a former bus garage in Shepherd's Bush in London. The factory team could assemble the prototype in three hours and 20 minutes under ideal conditions, meaning that constructing it in the field, in the dark, could be accomplished in roughly eight hours. For security reasons, the dummy LCTs were christened "Bigbobs", to distinguish from their cousins, the smaller inflatable rubber dummy assault landing craft (LCAs) known as "Wetbobs". The next question: did the Bigbobs look like the real thing?

So it was back to the test site. Each Bigbob required eight Army three-ton lorries or three ten-ton railway wagons. The crew reassembled the "Bigbob", placed it next to its genuine counterpart and took photos from the air. The resemblance was striking, but the phoney one looked too clean – until workmen tossed sump oil onto the sides and painted on rust marks.[31]

On 14 July, a lake in Windsor Great Park was chosen for training the building squads and erection team due to its excellent security control. Of course, since the lake was in a Royal Park, permission from King George VI was needed to use it, and a Mr Saville, Chief Agent for the Crown Lands, was charged with vouching for the integrity of the 30 workers on the Royal Estate. Military Police cordoned off the selected area and only a small gate at the side of the Wheatsheaf Hotel permitted entry. With all security issues resolved, and with badges and armed guards everywhere, the work began.

And then one of the security people spotted an amorous couple in *flagrante delicto* sprawled on an islet in the lake in full view of the top-secret QUICKSILVER project. Chaos and shouting ensued and soon the now fully-dressed couple faced official grilling. They were married – but not to each other – and were desperate to keep the liaison out of the tabloids or the police record. Compassion ruled and the various officials agreed to let them go with a stern warning and a threat of violation of the Official Secrets Act – for which, in time of war, a dank cell and a publicized treason trial at the Old Bailey might end in execution by hanging.

With the grateful couple escorted away, work proceeded, although not without some unfortunate fiascos on the part of the trainees. One of these involved the collapse of a funnel assembly, when the men dropped their tools to take a swim. To make matters worse, the funnel landed on John English. The Bigbob's assembly operation otherwise proceeded with efficiency and in the prescribed three-hour schedule. American Engineers arrived before dawn to handle storage and the dispatch of the Bigbob parts from the Royal Estate.

General Sir Frederick Morgan, Chief of Staff to the Supreme Allied Commander, approved plans for about 80 Bigbobs to be located at various shielded locations along the South Coast. American and British troops would handle launches, beginning in August. On the other hand, John English, the Cox's representative, found the whole ordeal, especially after the dummy LCT's smoke funnel debacle, to be a complete disaster. British Lieutenant-Colonel Peter White, commander of the two companies of the 24th Airfield Construction Group, Pioneer Corps, found the Americans, "cheerful…" and stated that they "… gave the British all the help they needed". However, the Army decided the project was not technical enough for the Royal Engineers and turned it over to Lieutenant-Colonel White and his Pioneers.

Although all the sites had stringent security measures in place, the village of Beaulieu, near Buckler's Hard (a cement pier extended into the water to aid launch and retrieval of boats), also became a hotbed of other secret goings-on. The Special Operations Executive (SOE) had established training facilities for agents who would be parachuted into the continent to support the Resistance against the Axis. Fighter airfields had also been constructed nearby. The area was divided into inner and outer zones and access was limited to people having National Registration Cards and approved tradesmen delivering supplies. In addition, homes with rooms overlooking the launching points would billet only officers in those rooms, which would be locked when not in use.[32]

Building the dummy LCTs and then transporting them to their respective harbours did not occur without a series of glitches and frustrations. Inexperienced assemblers struggled to work in the dark and due to high winds the Navy encountered difficulties in towing Bigbobs from their launching sites. While experimenting with Landing Craft Personnel (LCP - another form of landing craft), it was learned the Navy didn't have enough tug tows to take the Bigbobs to Beaulieu.

Nevertheless, by early September 75 Bigbobs were in place and ready for action. At this point the Army shifted its attention to Operation HARLEQUIN, the launching of 100 Wetbobs near the River Stour. Noting an increase of enemy reconnaissance planes in the area, the Allies decided to set up two Operations, STARKEY and WADHAM, as part of Operation FORTITUDE (see p. 79). They feverishly assembled mock army camps and embarkation points, including fake lighting. At the same time, to co-ordinate with the STARKEY Operation, the Army scheduled beach-landing exercises, but after several days of turbulent weather and high waves, a number of the Wetbobs were damaged. When the weather cleared, it was decided that Operation STARKEY would proceed as planned. In the pre-dawn hours of 9 September, a group of Bigbobs were towed out into the Channel accompanied by two warships, merchant ships, landing barges complete with troops and 72 fighter aircraft roaring overhead, plus assaults by Bomber Command – all directed at Calais. However, this array of Allied strength failed to impress the Germans enough to provoke out a counter-attack, and the ignored convoys and squadrons turned for home. Officials, discouraged by this turn of events, decided to cease both HARLEQUIN and WADHAM Operations soon after.

The Bigbobs were dismantled and returned to Watford, but not forgotten. In late September, after consulting with his company commanders, Colonel White wrote a detailed report on the most efficient method for scheduling and assigning workloads during Bigbob construction.

The document that he created became one of the most valuable when it came time to set up Operation QUICKSILVER the following year (see p. 86). One element of Operation FORTITUDE,

Operation QUICKSILVER, a subpart of FORTITUDE, was a strategic military deception designed to make the Germans believe the US Army would soon be landing at Pas-de-Calais after D-Day in Normandy. Dummy landing craft were built for British coasts and estuaries by movie studios and civilian wood shops using mostly civilian labour to deceive Hitler's forces.

QUICKSILVER covered props and settings. Bigbobs were called in to play once again, this time 100 would be added, modelled after the new Mark 4 LCTs, bringing a total of 315 craft. About 36 specially modified Bigbobs would actually resemble dummies to differentiate between those that appeared genuine to the enemy.

In addition, about 160 Wetbobs which had survived the STARKEY Operation would be employed, while about 150 new sturdier models were planned as well.

During the early months of 1944, a training camp for building the Bigbobs was established at Waldringfield, a small village near Ipswich and the River Deben. The construction logistics were similar to the original, with three teams handling the bow, midship and stern sections, and then bolting all three together, after which the funnel, mast and bow doors were added. The frame was covered with laced-on painted canvas sheets. They then slid the Bigbobs down the slipway into the river and placed the craft at their respective mooring buoys. All done in darkness, all completed in six hours.

Additional construction teams joined the group and by early April 1944, 700 men were billeted near the training site. At the same time, Colonel David Strangeways determined the construction locations for the Bigbob fleets: to Waldringfield was added Great Yarmouth, Lowestoft, Woolverstone Park, Dover and Folkestone.

Dover presented a small problem. The construction site could be seen from the cliffs above; spies observing activity would see troops building dummy craft. Large screens were built to mask the movements while still giving the impression of activity. Engineers reinforced and widened roads leading to the shore, to make it appear that preparations were afoot to accommodate heavily armoured vehicles.

Convoys of construction materials slated for the Bigbobs lumbered over country lanes until they reached a wooded area. Workmen unloaded the contents and hid them under hedgerows, then dozed in their trucks until daybreak. Meanwhile, under cover of darkness, construction crews worked throughout the night assembling yet one more landing craft. As one driver put it, "In the morning the completed LCT would be afloat and all that could be seen was a Jeep towing a harrow over the field to erase all tell-tale tracks ..."

By the time of the D-Day landings in June, about 300 dummy LCTs had been nosed into position by tugs on the east and south-east coast.

Allied deception tactics seemed to have no bounds. An Army encampment sprouted up along the River Orwell in Suffolk, including a guard house, tents, phoney vehicles and even a parade square. Night noises created a sense of a real camp and fake messages were sent between ship and shore.

The construction personnel took on the roles of seamen's duties. They played at fishing off the deck, hanging laundry, "painting" sides and sending messages via Aldis lamp. Oil burners provided special effects, producing occasional plumes of smoke. Mail bags, ammunition boxes and other stores were delivered daily. Small tankers arrived regularly and used oiling hoses to simulate refuelling operations. Both real and phoney LCTs often sailed and returned together. The deception worked so well that even Women's Royal Navy Service personnel at HMS *Woolverstone* believed that the Bigbobs were genuine British craft. When enemy aircraft flew overhead, local AA batteries fired at them, but avoided bringing any planes down, so that any photos taken by German pilots would reach intelligence offices. As it turned out, Bigbobs at Dover and Folkestone were hit by Nazi shore batteries based at Cap Gris Nez, but stayed stubbornly afloat. The Quicksilver teams finally disposed of them, allowing the Germans to tout their skills in inflicting severe damage on the Allied invasion fleet.

The enemy was further led astray by "Mandrel," a radar technology used by Lancaster bombers of 100 Group called the ABC Patrol, which flew back and forth along the enemy coast jamming the Germans' *Freya* and *Würzburg*, a version of radar. Another squadron of bombers threw out bundles of foil strips (called "Window") which caused strange echoes to appear on radar screens.

A couple of phoney attacks were set up on the Channel coast, again intended to turn German heads toward destinations other than Normandy. Operation TAXABLE involved a fleet of motor launches from Portsmouth heading toward Cap d'Antibes hauling low-flying balloons containing "Moonshines" (radar reflecting devices). A similar Operation, called GLIMMER sailed out of Dover, with Boulogne as their destination.

To add to the tangled web of deception, Operation TITANIC involved the creation of dummy uniformed parachutists outfitted with detonating fireworks that appeared as rifle fire. They were dropped at Yvetot, near Le Havre and Dieppe, St-Lô and Caen.

Days after the landings at Normandy, General Guingand – Montgomery's No. 2 – of the 21st Army Group messaged to Colonel Wills who commanded the 10th Worcesters that the fake landing craft would be most valuable if they could continue in this role. He wanted as much life and animation to be infused in them. Colonel Wills messaged back in early July, that overcoming the difficulties in keeping the Bigbob fleet intact in bad weather at Dover was nearly impossible without the use of powerful tugs, which were in short supply.

In the end, how effective was QUICKSILVER? Captured German intelligence reports seized by advancing Allied troops showed that the enemy believed there were at least 42 divisions of Allied forces and a fleet of 500 large landing craft assembled in south-east England, all set for an assault on Pas-de-Calais. In truth, only 15 divisions were set to go and no ships. Meanwhile, the Germans, who had accepted as true the whole Pas-de-Calais scenario, sent their 14th and 15th armies along with several Panzer divisions toward Fécamp, Boulogne and Dieppe, north-east of the Normandy beaches, away from the major assault. This helped the Allies end the battles in the vicinity of Caen and eventually hastened the capture of the deep-water port at Cherbourg.[33]

CHAPTER 10

FORTITUDE

So far, the deception operations for the cross-Channel invasion had been grouped in FORTITUDE SOUTH. In contrast, the fake 4th Army Group languished in the hilly wind and rain-swept inland areas of Northern Britain. Born from the need for a fake feint attack on the Norwegian coast, it consisted of only a few lines of text at the top of a blank manuscript. At best, it was a command backwater. But for those who respected FORTITUDE's wheels within wheels, such mis-directions were key. For Hitler, the Norway invasion menace was just such an additional distraction alongside the apparent Pas-de-Calais full attack (and both concealed the real threat to Norway). Pulling off the FORTITUDE NORTH deception, though, would need a certain genius.

Colonel R. M. "Rory" MacLeod, aged 52 and despite row upon row of medals on his First World War uniform, had been sidelined. On 3 March 1944, he was umpiring a war game on the grim Yorkshire Moors when he received a written order to report to Brigadier Richard Barker at SHAEF HQ soonest.

On arrival, expecting to be informed he would command a combat brigade on D-Day, he was told by Barker, "Rory, old boy, you have been selected to run a deception Operation for SHAEF from Scottish Command. You will travel to Edinburgh, and there you will represent an army which does not, in fact, exist." It would be hard to imagine how far down MacLeod's spirits plunged. Barker continued at length:

"By means of fake signals traffic, you will, however fool the Germans into believing that an army does exist, and what is more, that it is about to land in Norway and clear the Germans out of there. It is terrifically important that it should be a success."

General Andrew "Bulgy" Thorne, an officer who had served as military attaché in Berlin and was an acquaintance of many top Wehrmacht generals, was cast as the figurehead planner of this fictional Fourth Army Group. The Fourth would co-ordinate with Montgomery's 21st Army Group, and the planners running the notional First United States Army Group (FUSAG), which was aimed at the Pas-de-Calais deceptions.[34] MacLeod was notionally Thorne's deputy, but he would run the Scottish outfit. He was assured his fake command would be quickly pinpointed by very efficient Nazi "Y-Service" monitors, and their agents would hang on every wireless transmission.

Shown out of SHAEF's Norfolk House and bundled into a train, he soon found himself ensconced in rooms below the ramparts of Edinburgh Castle, looking down from its cliffside perch at the nearby tangle of Edinburgh's narrow lanes and across at the crowning hilltop called Arthur's Seat. From there, he would create his phantom Fourth Army Group and hoodwink Hitler.[35]

MacLeod swallowed his disappointment, plunged into staffing his headquarters with an over-age-for-combat collection of officers and set up a corps HQ at the ancient town of Stirling. From there, an army corps began to materialize, including the actual United States 15th Corps under the command of Major-General Wade H. Haislip. To establish communications between that corps in Ulster, a liaison officer joined MacLeod at Edinburgh Castle. Some of the postings were inadequate, since most officers lacked experience in setting up a wireless network. A quick message shot up to SHAEF's HQ solved that problem and soon he mustered eight officers and 24 radio operators whose presence now had to be explained to curious locals. MacLeod had no confidence that all the spies in Scotland had been scooped up by MI5.

To cover this sudden influx of non-combat military, rumours were spread suggesting a vast training exercise was underway across Scotland. MacLeod swore the lot to secrecy and explained their roles in the plot to deceive the Germans on the time and place of the upcoming D-Day assault, emphasizing how important FORTITUDE NORTH was to the success of those landings. He also pointed out the grim penalties for loose lips. The code-name for their work was SKYE.

MacLeod learned that FORTITUDE NORTH was at the mercy of SHAEF's ever-changing conception of the overall deception operation. This required constant scrutiny and appropriate Fourth Army changes to the radio scripts fed to the Germans. If that wasn't enough, the actual military units attached to the notional Fourth Army often failed to acknowledge the importance of the deception, or co-operated only when it was convenient for their training programs. Haislip's actual 15th Corps, which mustered the 2nd, 5th, and 8th Infantry Divisions was training in Northern Ireland for OVERLORD, but the Fourth Army script had the 15th Corps slated for "reinforcing" the attack on Norway by sailing from Belfast, Mercey, Rosyth and Invergordon. "Bulgy" Thorne's invasion force would embark from the well-known Scottish bays: the Firth of Clyde, and the Firth of Forth.

To add to the Fourth Army's "corps" in constant communication, which amounted to 250,000 men, a tactical air force and 250 tanks, MacLeod established support units such as: the 303rd Antiaircraft Regiment, the 87th Field Cash Office – soldiers did have to be paid – the Seventh Corps Postal Unit, a Film and Photographic section, the 405th Road Construction Company of the Royal Engineers and the 55th Field Dressing Station to treat casualties arriving from the Norway invasion. Besides these fictitious entities, the Double-Cross Committee jumped in with a series of faux German agents who reported seeing soldiers training in white winter cassocks and practising skiing on slippery grass slopes. Wireless requests for vehicle engine maintenance in cold weather were broadcast, as well as orders for Norwegian phrase books. "Ønsker du en candy, ung dame?" ("Would you like some candy, young woman?")

As the Fourth Army was shaping up, two German agents were captured as soon as they waded ashore from their seaplane in Moray Firth. They surrendered easily and offered themselves as double agents. Their codes and radios were aimed back at Germany with fake intelligence under the code-names, Mutt and Jeff. To spice up their story, a Russian officer was spotted by Mutt visiting Edinburgh Castle, suggesting a British-Russian combined Operation to clear the Germans out of Norway. Even the priceless British double agent, Garbo got in on the act. He created a crack agent named "Benedict", who proved to be a fount of bogus information with details down to the Fourth Army's new shoulder patch.

Actual shipping was gathered into the Scottish coast complete with RAF Spitfires flying "cover" for the armada, except, of course for that odd German recon plane who "managed to slip through". These RAF overflights apparently originated from one of the many bogus airfields where squadrons of rubber, stick and canvas fighters and bombers were badly camouflaged. The information coming from trusted sources in Scotland had German intelligence bewildered about the actual force gathering in Scotland. Nervous officers in the fractured German command structure chopped Allied division estimates, expecting Heinrich Himmler's SD (*Sicherheitsdienst* – the Nazi party's intelligence organization) to double the number of attacking forces, whatever it took to match whatever threats Hitler was pulling from his hat. Nobody – but nobody – wanted to be caught on the short end of a bad prediction (the sound of Schmeisser submachine guns echoing off execution walls was a constant reminder of the price for suspected treason).[36]

On the diplomatic side, FORTITUDE NORTH was bolstered by Operation GRAFFHAM , which began in late March 1944 with the recall to London of Victor Mallet, the British minister in Stockholm. The LCS plan to support the FORTITUDE NORTH deception consisted of creating a diplomatic crisis between Sweden and the Allies by expanding the list of current requests that the Allies were making on the neutral government of Sweden. These additional demands included:

1. The right of Allied aircraft to land at Swedish airfields and refuel after combat operations.

2. Permission to send British experts to consult Swedish

counterparts about the transportation of supplies between Norway and Sweden, should the Germans vacate Norway.

3. The right of the Allies to conduct survey and reconnaissance flights over Sweden.

As expected (and desired), Sweden at first rejected the demands. Mallet had been told by the LCS to drag out the discussions and make them last as long as possible. Information about the negotiations was conveyed to the *Abwehr* through a variety of means. These included a German spy in Stockholm with access to a Swedish intelligence officer who was unknowingly fed information by the LCS, and the seeding of diplomatic gossip, newspaper stories and editorials.

The LCS even played economic games with Sweden. This activity began with speeches made by U.S. Congressmen that stressed American resolve to deal severely with any neutral countries supporting Germany's war efforts. At this time Sweden was supplying Germany with iron ore, ball bearings and machine tools, all goods on which the Allies demanded embargos be imposed. The Allies then deliberately tampered with Stockholm's stock market to run up the price of Norwegian securities to further fuel investor speculation on the imminent invasion and liberation of Norway.

The deception of FORTITUDE NORTH was a complete success and tied up 27 German divisions for the defence of Norway and Denmark. Hitler not only prevented forces from leaving Norway to go to France, he actually reinforced Norway. By the late spring of 1944, in Norway alone huge military resources were stationed: 13 army divisions, 89,000 naval personnel, 58,000 Luftwaffe personnel, 6,000 SS and 12,000 paramilitary forces. With the threat of invasion never fully removed, the majority of these units would find themselves still in Norway at the end of the war, a diversion of resources which badly hit Germany's main war effort. One can only conjecture the number of Allied (and German) lives saved by making these forces unavailable for combat in France or Germany.[37]

To keep the guessing game going, the ever-resourceful Dudley Clarke and his A-Force con men floated a bogus invasion of the Bay of Biscay scheduled for 7 June 1944. Articles also appeared in magazines where "experts" confidently debated theories that the Allies would claw their way up to Germany through the Balkans. Not to be outdone, Fleet Street entered into the spirit, publishing endless technical photos and diagrams with captions, "We're Ready!" and "Giant Armada poised!"

By the spring of 1944, the results from MacLeod's in-depth work on creating the Fourth Army Group and FORTITUDE's earlier machinations with nervous, neutral Sweden coupled with certainty, provoked by Russian pressure, that there would be a second front, was bearing fruit. German intelligence became heavily loaded in their estimate of the coming invasion and, despite Hitler's distrust of his intelligence services, in late April, to Rory MacLeod's satisfaction, Berlin ordered the six Wehrmacht divisions in Norway to go on alert status and maintain it until further notice.

CHAPTER 11

THE DECEPTION SHELL-GAME – AMERICA WANTS IN

Americans are no strangers when it comes to deception. Their free-wheeling culture has always been fertile ground for the con-artist and the medicine show barker. American history is full of schemes, ploys, ruses and intrigues, so listening to the British go on about: "out-foxing the Desert Fox" in North Africa or floating a document-laden corpse to the Spanish shore, or even turning German spies into a "Special Means" group, and spreading fake intelligence to the Nazi Oberkommando der Wehrmacht (OKW) provoked a sense of envy. American invasion planners wanted a share in the deception action.

The idea of the European invasion turning into another Dieppe, or Dunkirk bloodbath was unthinkable. Back in the dark early days of the war, Winston Churchill determined the Britons would need more than pluck and fighting spirit to overcome the Nazi war machine. And so, the greatest hoax ever attempted was born.

FORTITUDE, OVERLORD, BODYGUARD, NEPTUNE – all the labyrinth of intertwining operations that made up the planning for the invasion of France – drew in the best and brightest of Britain's creative plotters. By 1943, Dudley Clarke had already created a plausible "order of battle" made up of mythical armies, corps, regiments, battalions, divisions and their complex tables of organization, real enough to be accepted by German Intelligence (see p. 39). A sprinkling of actual commanding officers, statistical inventories of armour and infantry assets, plausible air force squadrons and functioning communications networks had been added to the fictional groups to make them feel real to the Germans. This phantom reality inflated the size of actual British forces, allowing ghost divisions to pin down Nazi armour and their confused officers, while an actual attack came brewing up on the enemy's flanks – or an entire notional blocking armoured division simply melted away.

And now, that order of battle's most crucial test was near, the cross-Channel amphibious invasion of occupied France and breaking out into the German Third Reich. Everyone expected it. How does one hide an invasion? One doesn't. It was enough just to convince Adolf Hitler that he knew where the invasion would come.

The shaky co-operation between British and American concepts of deception warfare had barely begun to come together. The American side of the British-run FORTITUDE was chugging along in late 1943. The six-part QUICKSILVER and its dummy landing craft construction, Double XX and Special Means' fake wireless broadcasts were building the credibility with German Intelligence of the existence of two faux Army groups: FUSAG, lurking in the south of England and the British Fourth Army in Scotland.

An American deception program was needed. It would have to use what the British had, but also carry beyond the strategic to follow American fighting units into the European Theatre of Operations (ETO) as a tactical application – on call as a Top-Secret adjunct to the combat troops.

General Jake Devers commanded the Headquarters of the American Army in Europe (ETOUSA) at a time when British-run Operation COCKADE, the fake invasion of France in 1943 had flopped. It demonstrated that there were not enough troops in Britain to sustain such an attack.[38]

Dudley Clarke was preparing to convince ETOUSA to allow his A-Force to run the American deception program. Seizing on the British COCKADE fumble, Devers called in American Colonel William ("Billy") Harris as deception officer for the American European Theatre. Harris's first task was to write a report on what was needed for the tactical trickery portion of the OVERLORD operation.

The deception unit emerging from Harris's report had the ability to simulate one corps containing one infantry division and one armoured division, by using prefabricated dummies and suitable fake radio communications. General Omar Bradley, who arrived in England to command the First Army, went over the report with Devers and General Daniel Noce, questioning the viability of the portable dummies. Further examination of British decoys and dummies by the War Department's Joint Security Control suggested more realistic designs. Both Devers and Bradley approved the deception unit's new stagecraft and expanded it to include one armoured and two infantry divisions. Their assembling and training base would be Camp Forest in Tullahoma, Tennessee, under the command of the Second Army. The unit was activated on 20 January 1944. In this way, following Clarke's British model, the U.S. military created a "Ghost Army" of their own.

On the Table of Organization (TO), this curiously composite orphan was blandly listed as the 23rd Headquarters Special Troops, encompassing: The 244th Signal Company (Special), the 603rd Engineer Camouflage Battalion (Special), the 406th Engineer Combat Company (Special) and the 3132nd Signal Service Company (Special).[39]

The Ghost Army's role was as a top-secret mobile group assigned wherever a deception was needed, a sleight-of-hand required, or an army of 30,000 soldiers had to be impersonated. The vanished combat unit was replaced by a handful of artists, actors, carpenters, electricians, sound trucks, rubber and pasteboard tanks, inflatable artillery, a cardboard air force and bogus radio communications. In most cases, this mythical band's job was to draw fire and attention from the Germans while the actual fighting force appeared – as if by magic – on that enemy's unprotected flank. Other operations required them to sound like rolling thunder at the enemy's front, a boiling mass of guns and tanks, surging at the leash behind the black of night, or hidden by a billowing cloud of fog, *"Life is but a walking shadow ... full of sound and fury, signifying ... nothing..."*[40]

Colonel Harry L. Reeder was selected to command the 23rd, to his crushing chagrin. After his years in active service, he yearned for a combat command at the head of an armoured infantry unit and the heat of battle. Instead, he was saddled with a collection of apparent non-combatants, intellectual draft dodgers who called themselves "artistes" whom he had to turn into soldiers for ... what? Not even the War Department knew anything about deception. There were no manuals, no guidelines and nobody on his assigned "staff" knew anything about tricking Germans. Most of the enlisted men were smarter than most of his officers and stood around like sheep at the early roll-calls. Whipping this creative mob into a military operation would take all of Reeder's experience.

After hacking away for three months, the 23rd's Table of Organization listed 28 officers, one warrant officer and 92 enlisted men, or one officer for every three-and-a half-troops in the HQ unit ... or roughly, considering all the revolving-door transfers. Since Washington knew nothing about deception, the TO was accepted without changes. Oddly, the unit had an oversupply of West Point graduates who usually gravitated to combat commands where advancement up the rank ladder was faster. This list, top-heavy with smart people was some indication of the importance given to deception tactics as demonstrated by the British and amphibious applications over previous campaigns.

Colonel Clifford G. Simenson, selected for the operations and training job in the 23rd, reacted to his appointment much as Reeder had: "What have I done wrong?" Without any guidance from American upper echelons – or even his own commanding officer – Simenson sought any outside help he could find (which meant the British). Secrecy clouded information at every turn. With no written material available, all training was verbal and applied to paper later. One break helped the 23rd's Training Officer; the Army Specialized Training Programs (ASTPs) were being phased out to provide more combat soldiers. The 23rd was flooded with refugees from this batch of bright minds who had joined up to use their unique skills and now faced being shipped into the ground-pounding grind of the regular military.

Created at the end of the war, this map shows the Ghost Army's routes and operations. The 1,100 men belonging to 23rd Headquarters Special Troops were active in Normandy, northern France, Rhineland, Ardennes and central Europe from April 1944 until June 1945.

When Simenson launched his enlistees into military drill and training, he made a discovery: instead of relying on constant repetition to drive the lessons home, these sharp recruits picked up training quickly. They treated the military's mind-numbing drill and procedures as just something new to learn.

Camouflage came to mind first when organizing the 23rd's capability and this component came with the invaluable 603rd Engineer Camouflage Battalion (Special). Training at Fort George G. Meade, Maryland, the 603rd had already been in operation for two years before being incorporated into the 23rd. Its ranks included some of the best and brightest artists available from New York and Philadelphia. Fashion icon Bill Blass and photographer Art Kane headed a list of equally skilled commercial artists alerted to the enlistment opportunity through the Art Students League and a camouflage course taught at New York University. Theatre set-designer George Diestel and commercial artist George Martin had joined up along with artists Arthur Singer, Ellsworth Kelly, Arthur Shilstone and Bernie Bluestein from the Cleveland Institute of Art.

Bernie, a tall, muscular twenty-year-old, had been a student at the Cleveland school in 1943. At that time the school's curriculum focused on practical aspects of art, training students for careers in the applied arts. During the Second World War, courses such as medical drawing, map-making and camouflage were added. Bernie recalled:

"One day an instructor told me, 'you're about to be drafted. The government has set up a program to get enlisted men into a certain outfit of the army. You'd have to take a camouflage course.'"

Bernie attended the class for a term and learned about the rudiments of camouflage – including how to disguise an airfield – and later joined the 603rd Engineers Camouflage Battalion. After basic training in Fort Hayes, Ohio, Bernie joined the 603rd at Fort George Meade. Bluestein recalled that at that time the dummy tanks were constructed with wooden slats:

"We made them light so we could carry them and the slats formed the object we were making, whether it was a gun or plane or something else to give solidity to it. They were covered with burlap and then we painted them camouflage. Some [tanks] didn't even have treads on them; they were pretty crude. Later – don't know exactly when – the government said they we're going to build them out of neoprene rubber and make them collapse; easier to transport and mass produce than the wooden things."[41]

Bernie was in good company; in all, the 603rd TO had an above-average IQ of 119. As of 14 April 1944 it consisted of 28 officers and two warrant officers, who commanded 361 enlisted men divided into a Headquarters Company, four separate companies (A, B, C and D) and a 12-man medical department (MED Det).

The 23rd had the pick of the best brains and a very high priority rating for equipment procurement, "A-2-a-0.1". What they wanted, they got. Decoys had been a matter of conjecture. Hard-nosed cavalry types were suspicious of fake M-4 Sherman tanks that could be inflated. Almost everyone's experience with photos of decoy tanks had only been with the early British models. These balloon-like models looked good to a camera peering down from 3,000 feet (900 metres), but at 500 yards (450 metres), facing a wary German anti-tank battalion, it was another matter.

The Engineer Board set about testing two more sophisticated Shermans. The model supplied by General Outdoor Advertising Company was based on a hinged folding metal frame with panels, linked together with pins. The tanks were assembled and taken down ten times. The metal frame Sherman proved too fragile at the hinges and folds and the linking pins could be lost. It was too heavy and slower to deploy than the rubber model. Since the tanks and other decoys tested were for a top-secret project, submitting manufacturers were told they were for "target practice," which suggested a controlled transport and set-up situation, not a live battlefield. The new inflatable tanks had a static profile measuring

18 feet (5.5 metres) long and seven and a half feet (2.3 metres) high to the turret top, suitable for viewing as close as 500 yards (450 metres) in daylight. Whether alone, or scattered among real tanks, the result was convincing.

The neoprene rubber tank was built at U.S. Rubber's Alice Mill in Woonsocket, Rhode Island, and a consortium of companies including: U.S. Rubber, Goodyear, and the Scranton Lace Curtain Manufacturing Company, in Scranton, Pennsylvania. This rubber tank was quite upscale from the British original, utilizing connected inflatable components, each with its own air tube. If a wing was punctured, only the wing panel had to be patched – in an emergency, sometimes with chewing gum.[42]

According to Bernie Bluestein, "We had to rehearse. Had to learn how to carry them in our truck; dismantle them very fast, blow them up and install them. All had several inflation points. We used gasoline air compressors and hoped the enemy wouldn't be that close to hear the motor sounds." [43]

The 244th Signal Company (Special) acted as the 23rd's wireless communication team. They would be added in Wellesbourne, Warwickshire, England where the company was organized as a unit and its activation made retroactive back to 7 April 1944.[44]

Six officers and 193 enlisted men from the "unassigned" pool were transferred to the 23rd on 22 June 1944. During the search for the best men for this signal unit, more than 40 per cent of the original choices were transferred elsewhere. Five new officers and 100 enlisted men were added to fill the depleted ranks. The 244th was renamed Signal Company, Special, 23rd Headquarters Special Troops.

The Signal Company was responsible for distributing deception messages for transmission and for inter-company communications and received a large number of SCR radios with ranges from 25 to 100 miles (40 to 160 kilometres) and short-range transceivers for artillery spotters and unit combat simulations. Good mimics with a flair for the theatrical and an ear for accents were valuable assets. A load of 63 miles (100 kilometres) of comm wire was also allocated to their mobile units. Officials believed that wire stringing under combat conditions would keep "intelligent, theatrical mimics" grounded in their more mundane military role in the team.

Company A of the 293rd Engineer Combat Battalion was carved away to form the 406th Combat Engineers section of the 23rd on 4 April 1944. These troops – the best company in the 293rd – would handle all combat needs of the 23rd as well as running added bulldozers, water filtration plants and manning mobile .50 and .30 calibre heavy machine guns for self-defence mounted on Jeeps and other vehicles. The unit, consisting of five officers and 175 enlisted men was commanded by the highly regarded Captain George Rebh, a graduate of the West Point Class of January 1943.

The combined 23rd Headquarters Special Troops endured Colonel Reeder's grumpy military outlook at Camp Forrest and produced a number of schemes to fool the Germans with camouflage and radio transmissions. As training progressed, Reeder's opinion of his command improved, but he was still close-mouthed when it came to keeping his troops informed. Despite this under-communicative oversight, creative soldiers like Lieutenant Frederick Fox kept ideas flowing for radio trickery and camouflage stunts to keep the Germans guessing. Fox's Princeton dramatic studies and flair for theatre set the operational tone for the "23rd Travelling Road Show" – a name that stuck.

The most sophisticated notional weapon to be aimed at the Germans was a rich palette of sonic illusions. The master of that art was the 3132nd Signal Service Company, Special, assigned to further enhance the 23rd's Signal Company capabilities. Their craft deserves special recognition, both for its advanced audio technology and for its combat applications from the 3132nd's arrival in Europe in August 1944, just after D-Day to the campaigns that followed to the borders of Germany.

CHAPTER 12

EVERY STAGE CAN USE AN ORSON WELLES

Larger than life, sophisticated, bold, entrepreneurial, a master director, brilliant performer, writer, designer, casting director, erratic, intimidating, impatient, alcoholic, con man, and a leader of men when he turned up the heat – all that was Colonel Hilton Howell Railey. In the specialized world of sonic deception during World War II, Railey was the master of the medium.

Hilton Railey had made himself useful in pre-war military circles, including military intelligence, until he was re-activated as a lieutenant colonel and chief of the Planning and Training Branch responsible for coastal defences. His quick grasp of technology and leadership ability made him a natural choice for the War Department Planning and Training Board in September 1942. His gift for words – and a report critical of Army morale – landed him in front of the Joint Chiefs where he served as secretary and executive officer.

At this point, coincidence brought him into Douglas Fairbank's orbit and introduced him to the concept of sonic deception. The war-game "Battle of Sandy Hook" (see p. 96) was fresh on the demonstration books. Railey eagerly embraced Fairbanks' sonic deception package. When the Navy moved its sonic operations to Fort Bradford, the army established their Army Experimental Station (AES) at Fort Hancock on 4 June 1943, passing the facility from the Army Ground Forces to the Chief of the Signal Corps under Railey's command.

While the Navy had fully embraced the sonic deception concept, ordering 30 record-playback field units for naval amphibious applications, the Army only requested one to take apart and improve for the very different requirements of land warfare. The Navy units, initially, were battery-pack powered, worked off record platters on turntables, and were far too cumbersome to deal with highly mobile land transport over bumpy roads. Also, the Navy was keen to begin training immediately with the collection of technically basic equipment. They later switched over to the more durable and audio-improved wire recorders.

It turned out Fort Hancock was not a good location for recording and playing back sounds; there was too much activity and background noise in the area. Railey chose instead Pine Camp in Upper New York State, now named Fort Drum. It had Lake Ontario at hand for over-water testing, wooded areas and the Wheeler-Sack airstrip for bringing in equipment and men.

Beefing up, simplifying and improving quality took precedence with Railey. When the Army Experimental Station had moved to Pine Camp, the engineers of Division 17 of the National Defence Research Committee came up with an improved sound projection system. First, they downsized the Navy's "junior heater" 500-watt speaker complex – a dozen metal driver horns arrayed in a metal grid. The new system used 250 watts to project audio effects through six 15-inch (38-centimetre) "direct radiator" speakers framed in a 240-pound (110-kilogramme) weatherproof box with flared sides to focus projection.

Sound "presence" was also improved – when moving the sound of a rolling tank between speaker arrays, the stereo sound spanned the set-apart arrays, simulating the illusion of movement. This effect was complemented by recording a moving tank circling the microphone out at 100 feet (30 metres) rather than passing from left to right, which would have created an unwanted doppler effect from speaker to speaker. As in modern stereophonic sound systems, Bell Labs simulated an enveloping sound, making it difficult to pin-point any particular sound source.

Besides the technical aspects of sonic warfare, there was always the "show business" aspect. Without nuanced application of battlefield sounds, there was no illusion, there was no visualization of actual combat assets. Making use of the high-fidelity reproduction of tanks and armour moving into a location, the motors grumbling, transmission whining, suspension jolting in and out of potholes, meant all had to be "played into" position. Manipulation of the volume, panning the sound between heater speakers to suggest arrival and parking, unloading, and accompanying small utility vehicles, towing chains, idling engines, the whir of a rotating turret, and the slam of an artillery breech block – all these sounds combined to create a three-dimensional sound portrait. This portrait required an audio artist-engineer. If the armoured company was moving on to take position for infantry support or into an assembly area, the assets then had to be "played out" with starting engines, clunking gear levers, slamming hatches, the revving of engines, the clank and squeal of tank treads over bogie wheels. A light hand on the audio rheostat and a vivid visual imagination were needed to move an armoured unit across the enemy's front.

Shunning the record turntable used in the early days by the Navy in relatively stable boats, Bell Labs also lessened the chances of a needle skipping over platters on mud-rutted roads, or shell concussion vibrations. Instead, they adapted a civilian record-playback system that had been in use for years, the wire recorder. Invented in 1899 and improved up through the 1930s, the recorder used magnetic stainless-steel wire. One of its more visible commercial uses was aboard the high speed, 1934 Burlington Zephyr articulated passenger train. Conductors would swap wire spools with pre-recorded radio shows, concerts and sports events like the Dempsey-Tunney boxing championship which were piped through the coaches' speakers.[45]

The recorder's wire was .0006-inch (0.015mm) thick and moved over the playback heads at five feet per second (1.5 m/s). Stored in an interchangeable magazine, the two-mile (three-kilometre) long spool ran for 30 minutes. Each "heater" system in the field used two wire recorders to extend the playing time if needed, or interchange back and forth between the two. If the wire broke, a technician needed only to repair the break by tying the wire in a knot and holding a lit match underneath to melt the wire into its former continuous bond.

In collaboration with the Brush Development Company of Cleveland, Ohio, Bell Labs produced the KS-12009 rugged, basic playback system. Dubbed the PE-75 by the army, this brute was

As well as visual deception, sonic deception was used to misdirect the German army. Shown here is the speaker matrix cranked into position from its hiding place inside the half-track.

powered, not by a battery, but a Kohler gasoline generator pushing out two-and-a-half kilowatts of electric power.

At Pine Camp, additional effects were recorded into a sound library: truck and jeep noise; bridge building; bulldozers; artillery tractors; any activity that could be dubbed off three turntables into four wire recorders apiece. They could edit any sound programs required for a specific deception – mix-and-match – never letting the Germans hear a re-run.

Besides playing effects, the sonic team had a mobile weather station and two Air Force weather men. Their instrumentation measured barometric pressure, wind direction, force and humidity to determine optimum conditions and the correct angle of projection, direction and volume. On a clear night over water, they could send sound effects over fifteen miles (24 kilometres). At night, an inversion layer was suspended about ten feet (three metres) above the ground – appearing in the early morning as a "fog". Normally, however, the sonic teams rarely tried to project their programs more than 6,000 yards (5.5 kilometres).

Pine Camp's wooded isolation made it perfect for rehearsals. When the AES formally moved in during February 1943, its main job was the formation of the 3132nd Signal Service Company, achieved on 1 March 1944. The company comprised three basic elements: a headquarters platoon, three sonic platoons and a chemical platoon.

The three sonic platoons were each issued with five "sonic cars" – M3A1 half-tracks and a standard half-track for a command vehicle. These armoured hybrids were half tank and half lorry – lorry tyres on the front wheels and rubber treads running on bogies beneath the rear payload. As soon as their cars arrived with that fresh new half-track smell, they were stripped down and customized. The payload consisted of the "heater" sound system in steel cabinets, shock-proof mountings and a geared system to raise and swivel the loudspeaker matrix with a hand-crank called the "coffee grinder". A custom canvas cover hid the speakers when they were not needed. When cranked up into position, the sonic cars could reveal: a squadron of tanks crossing the front; engineers building a bridge; lorries labouring up a hill, motorboat engines crossing a river; a variety of combat sounds of a regiment, a division or a corps on the move.

"We only had sonic half-tracks with us during these missions," Bernie said. "We came in the evening, in the dusk where the Germans couldn't see us – only hear our effects that sounded like the whole world was filled with army vehicles, equipment; all kinds of sound. We even did some things like practising how to get boats into the water and out of the water. We had motorboat sounds even, so they thought we were practising."

The equipment was worked on and stored in the Wheeler-Sack airplane hangar; their existence was Top Secret. When en route to operations, they looked like any half-track. It was imperative that the Germans never capture a sonic car intact. To assure this outcome, two containers carried onboard held eight blocks of M-1 explosives and one M-2 block triggered by an 18-inch (45-centimetre), waterproof detonation fuse located under the driver's seat. Once lit, the driver and any passengers had fifteen seconds to make their dramatic exit.[46]

Most covert troop or armour movements that might be visually detected by an enemy observer were traditionally obscured by an "oil-fog" smoke screen provided by a 3132nd chemical half-track. This man-made fog smelled like gasoline exhaust, which reinforced the moving armour illusion. Observable distance from the enemy was an important factor in fog or audio projection. Testing proved the range of the current sound reproduction was measured in thousands of yards – unlike the naval offshore deceptions that needed closer smoke screens due to their more exposed proximity to beach defences.

The 3132nd chemical car command was reduced in priority since most 3132nd programs were mostly run at night. The reassigned troops from the chemical unit were repurposed as a security unit needed to protect all the physical deceptions from discovery by nosy civilians or German spies. It was commanded by Lieutenant Dick Syracuse, who had experience learned in the Chemical Warfare Corps. That training was quickly supplemented by learning how to manage his men as the unit's eyes and ears to keep wandering locals and German line-crossers in civilian clothes away from the deception materials. They also checked for any dummy anomalies (deflations, placements, etc.) that might draw a second look from a Nazi aerial recon pilot peering down at American positions.

No collection of sophisticated weapon systems was useful without an equally smart and motivated crew to extract the maximum effect from the weapons. The enlistees chosen for the 3132nd had passed through the abandoned Army Specialized Training Programs and were both bright and motivated – if they had the right officers – resulting in 56 per cent of their assigned officers washing out. Possibly, this high attrition was caused by demanding too much basic military skills and not enough showmanship from their sonic commands. After all, each sonic team was an act unto itself, crafted by self-motivated perfectionists who survived by their wits and relished conning the Germans. The 3132nd wanted flair, not spit-and-polish West Point clones.

CHAPTER 13

"GARBO" THE ONE-MAN PHANTOM SPY NETWORK

It was imperative for the success of OVERLORD that a deception plan be developed in parallel in order to persuade the OKW that their Führer's brilliant strategy was correct. Hitler needed to be convinced that to crush the invaders back into the sea he must stack most of his heaviest, nastiest armour and infantry forces with the 15th Army in Pas-de-Calais.

At the 1943 Quadrant Conference in Quebec, the Allied sea, land and air force planners were shown Morgan's final plan for the actual invasion at the Baie de la Seine in Normandy between the Cotentin peninsula and the port of Le Havre. This bit of coast allowed for five attack beaches: two for the Americans and three for the British, plus a deep-water harbour at Cherbourg on the tip of the peninsula for re-supply and additional troop landings. To make these landings succeed, two great leaps of faith were needed at the outset: absolute, iron-bound secrecy; and a method of re-supply beyond the point where the troops moved inland after the invasion beaches were secured.

The first part, secrecy had been partially achieved by 1943 through the efforts of MI5's running OPERATION FORTITUDE, detaining every resident German spy who tried to transmit to the Fatherland, unaware that the British had broken the *Abwehr* hand-sent code. The geographic fact that Britain was an island helped seal up entry and exit points, with a vigilant Home Guard keeping watch on open beach landing areas. The captured German spies now worked for British intelligence, courtesy of the Double-Cross Committee, who also employed a man called "Garbo".

On 6 June 1984, a short, balding man stood and gazed over the acres of crosses in the Colleville-sur-Mer cemetery near the shores of the Normandy coast. Tear droplets edged down his cheeks. "I could have done so much more," he whispered.

He wasn't a general, or a statesman or a national hero.

His name was Juan Pujol. He had fought in the Spanish Civil

War against Franco's Fascists, escaped capture and in 1940 worked as an unassuming hotel manager in Madrid. But at the height of World War II, he vanished into an identity known to the Allies as code-name "Garbo". In the days before and after D-Day, he pulled off one of the greatest deceptions in history. This is a fraction of his amazing story that helped save the Normandy invasion, and the very existence of the Ghost Army.

When the Germans drove their tanks into Poland, on 1 September 1939, Pujol knew he had to stop Adolf Hitler, a man he described as "a maniac, an inhuman brute".

As Denmark, Norway, Belgium, Holland and France fell to the Germans in the spring of 1940, and the British hobbled back from the bloodbath at Dunkirk, Pujol decided to serve the Allied cause in whatever way he could. On the positive side, he possessed a vivid imagination and felt certain he would use his talents best as a spy for the British. There was only one problem. He found it was nearly impossible to convince the British embassy in Madrid of his value, mainly because England had hoped to keep Spain as neutral as possible in the early days of the war. They didn't want any Spaniards muddying the waters.[47]

That rebuff left Pujol starting his career with the German *Abwehr*. At the very least he could obtain bits of Nazi intelligence and pass these off to the British when they eventually hired him. When he approached the German embassy in Madrid to offer his "services" as a spy, he was met with much less resistance. It took a few meetings plus a fair amount of charming play-acting to show the Germans that he wasn't just any fly-by-night, run-of-the-mill espionage agent. But he still needed to be in London.[48]

Out of desperation, Pujol's wife Araceli decided to intervene and met a few times with the American naval attaché. She produced a fake message written in invisible ink by a man she claimed to be a German spy who was staying at her boarding house. After using invisible ink developer to uncover the message, she revealed her husband was the so-called German spy, proving he had an inside path to the *Abwehr* operation. Startled, they realized that the man they had had summarily dismissed for so many months was none other than a spy – Arabel – which they had been aware of but unable to locate.[49]

On 1 May 1942, Pujol was at last settled in London, and soon after met Tommy Harris, the MI5 operative and Desmond Bristow, the officer for MI6. Pujol now needed an MI5 code-name, and, as with others in the spy network, the label was chosen to reflect his character. His greatest talent – the ability to easily assume another identity and play it to the hilt – led to MI5 baptizing him "Garbo," after the famous actress.[50]

Still, the XX Committee had to proceed slowly, as they made sure that Garbo spoon-fed the Germans just enough correct information mixed in with his expansive tales. It was vital that nothing should shake the Germans' confidence in Pujol's ability to provide increasingly valuable data.

Garbo had created a gaggle of phoney German double agents who roamed the English villages and seaside military operations and reported on hangar locations, barrage balloons, numbers of sentries, etc. His letters on their findings were forwarded on to Lisbon. Obviously, his letters ostensibly only passed on chatty family news and affections. Garbo wrote the real messages between the lines in invisible ink, in accordance with the Nazis' complex instructions.

Garbo's first real assignment was in concealing preparations in 1942 for Operation TORCH, the planned Allied invasion of North Africa. The Allies needed to feed Germany's preoccupation with a possible Norway invasion so that as many troops as possible were diverted northward. But first, Pujol had another concern. His "agent", in Liverpool was positioned to observe Allied movements heading toward the Mediterranean. If that agent missed seeing British military activity in the area, it would compromise Pujol's relationship with the *Abwehr*. Garbo and Harris devised a scenario in which the agent was suffering from a debilitating illness and needed surgery. But Pujol said he could replace him with additional agents in Scotland where activity and troop buildup had increased. [51]

The Germans rose to the bait, ordering Pujol to move more people to Wales and the Isle of Wight to see what they could find. Garbo reported back that the Allies had ambitious plans for a double strike targeting France and Norway.

He sent out mostly real facts that had little value, with some made-up information, until gradually the fake information outweighed the true. Garbo sent over 500 messages from the beginning of 1944 until D-Day. He reported on the placement of trucks, jeeps and tanks; evidence of the Second Army, the Eighth Army Air Force, etc. The idea was to report observations and let the Germans draw their own conclusions.

Pujol and Harris did all they could to lead the Germans into believing there would be two assaults. One of Garbo's agents reported activity in the northern British ports. Another invented character – Pujol's alleged lover in the War Ministry – claimed that they were only practice for the real thing which would take place some time later. Pujol said no, the attack would happen within a few hours. Of course, it didn't. This was only early May. And in truth these were rehearsals.

However, during another actual rehearsal, Exercise Tiger at Slapton Sands in Devon, German patrol boats came upon and attacked landing craft, causing severe loss of life for the Allies as well as destroying Sherman DD amphibious tanks and LST transports. Garbo blamed this surprise on his stumbling agents, but even then the Germans shared his frustration without calling him to task.[52]

Patton's Third Army, now attached to FUSAG (see p. 127), supposedly moved east to ready itself for its D-Day participation. In truth, personnel, and military equipment stayed put. Messages were sent using scrambled text that indicated the army was setting up in South-east England. Double agents reported tank officers,

FUSAG regiments and battalions chatting back and forth. Germany, meanwhile, kept track of these "movements", shifting pins and flags around on maps as they received reports.

Garbo's subagents had spotted FUSAG insignias (a black Roman numeral I on a blue pentagon) which he had mentioned to the Germans earlier) in areas around the coastline. They also reported squadrons departing from areas closer to Calais. The bombings of Calais were real, again reinforcing the Pas-de-Calais scenario. Garbo also told the *Abwehr* that he had been asked to work for the Political War Executive, charged with handling black propaganda. The Madrid office gave its approval, after which Garbo gave the Germans leaflets stating that the Allies would land in Normandy, leading Germany to believe it a ruse and that Calais was the real target.[53]

Strangeways had told Garbo earlier, neither Normandy nor Calais should be mentioned. Let Germany fill in the blanks. Hitler couldn't ignore the possibility of Normandy as a target. But Garbo insisted that what would be seen at Normandy should be interpreted as a feint – the Germans should ignore the fuss, the armies and the weaponry.

There were indications the deception was working. The Allies intercepted a message from the Japanese ambassador in Berlin to officials in Tokyo to the effect that Hitler believed the Allies would order diversionary attacks in northern Europe and south-western France as well as Normandy or Brittany, but that the true second front would be along the Channel. So, it was working. Hitler saw Normandy as only a sideshow; the real attack would occur elsewhere, most likely around Calais.[54]

Late on 5 June, Garbo sent an urgent message to Madrid agents advising them to have an operator listening at 0300 GMT. His Agent 3 had a message that he could only reveal when he arrived in London about 11.30 p.m. At 3.00 a.m., and with Eisenhower's permission, Garbo planned to pass on to the Germans the news he had been rehearsing for over a year: The invasion had begun. The storm-tossed Channel had calmed to a nasty chop and, against all nervous advice, Eisenhower had said, "Let's Go."

What Garbo did not say was that the troop transports, battleships, destroyers, landing craft, fighter planes and bombers, 20,000 vehicles and Operation NEPTUNE's 120,000 troops were already well on their way. The message would reach the Third Reich three-and-a-half hours after the launch; far too late for the Germans to mount a full-blown counter attack.[55]

And yet, in the early morning hours of 6 June, when it came time to send Garbo's message – no one at the *Abwehr* acknowledged Garbo's call sign. No operator responded until 8.00 a.m. Garbo assumed his usual role of the high-ranking agent frustrated with his low-level *Abwehr* colleagues:

"I am very disgusted as ...I cannot accept excuses or negligence," he complained.

He went on to say that three days ago his agent 4 had observed cold rations and vomit bags again being given to the Canadian Division which had left camp. Americans had arrived there as well.

The Germans believed that the invasion was underway, but that operations in Normandy were only a diversion. In truth, at that moment the Allies were already wading through the water and struggling up the sands on Operation NEPTUNE's five landing beaches. Deception was replaced by the raw courage and dogged endurance of the Allied combat soldier.

After Hitler received Garbo's message, he went with his first instinct, and ordered the Panzers back to Calais to be ready for the full-blown forces when they attacked. Then, reassured, he went back to sleep.

The German OKW, meanwhile, was literally frozen with indecision and frustration through the first hours of D-Day. Just long enough.

Months after the Normandy landings, the true worth of Garbo's operation became clearer. Both the *Abwehr* and Allied military heaped high praise on the Spanish spy. The Allies claimed his creation and execution were "the greatest double cross operation of the war" and "stranger than any fiction". Ironically, he was still regarded by the Germans as one of their top agents.

It was time for Garbo to disappear. MI5 managed to get him arrested, and then released. Even though their agent had been freed, the *Abwehr* panicked, but Garbo was too valuable to lose now. MI5's plan had worked perfectly.

No one in Berlin suspected him and on 29 July 1944, Pujol was informed that he had been awarded the Iron Cross by the Führer himself, for his "extraordinary services" to Germany.

By August 1944 other *Abwehr* agents had surrendered to the Allies, and if Germany got word that Garbo had not been arrested, it would prove he was a double agent. Garbo left London and told the Germans he was hiding in a farm in Wales, with another cast of made-up characters. In December 1944, Pujol was awarded the MBE, Member of the Most Excellent Order of the British Empire.

Pujol became the only agent to receive honours from both the British *and* the Germans.[56]

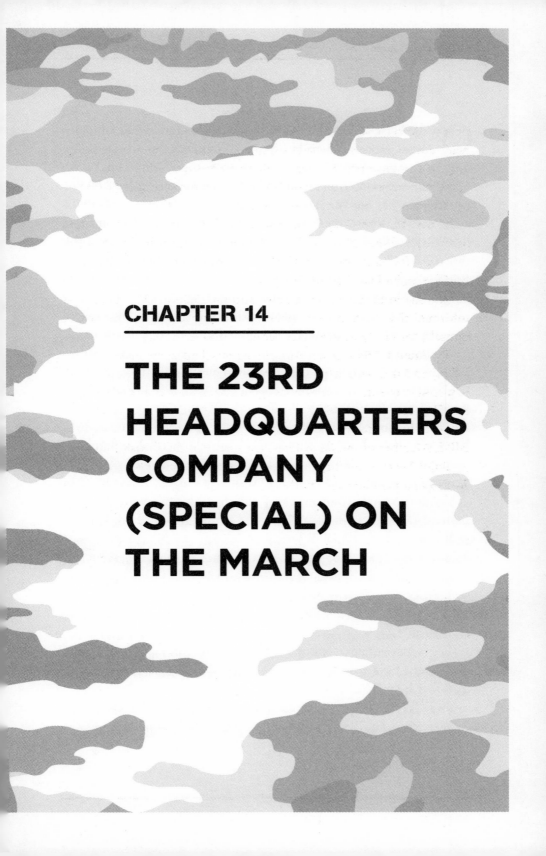

CHAPTER 14

THE 23RD HEADQUARTERS COMPANY (SPECIAL) ON THE MARCH

On 21 April 1944, all units of the 23rd Headquarters Company Special Troops – their latest official designation – departed by train from Camp Forest to arrive at Camp Kilmer, New Jersey, on 22 April. Nine days later, an advance party of eleven officers and NCOs departed by car for the New York Port of Embarkation (NYPOE) in Brooklyn, where they boarded United States Army Transport (USAT) 592, the USS *Henry Gibbins* to prepare for assembling the entire 23rd HQ unit. On 2 May, everyone – with Bernie Bluestein among them – showed up for the departure to England, which left the pier the next day to no fanfare, no cheering crowd.

The *Gibbins* was "... a good clean ship" modelled after American President class luxury liners. Its accommodations – considering it was a commandeered troop transport – were superb. Since an advance party of seven officers and NCOs headed by Colonel Reeder left for England by plane, Lt-Colonel Frederick Day assumed command of the shipboard complement.

The advance party was searching for information unavailable in the States. Lt-Colonel Simenson, for example, needed to have his command familiar with all forms of German intelligence gathering in order to confuse and neutralize these. The signal officer needed to know the power and range of German signal intelligence, and acquaint himself with signal deception attempted by the British and Americans previous to D-Day as well as the radio set-ups and signature policy of American corps and divisions already in the ETO.

To their chagrin, most of the information they needed was guarded by high security classifications and as if that weren't enough, the 23rd didn't have access to "Eyes-Only" intelligence. Furthermore, the British Isles was alive with pre-D-Day preparations and – the greatest irony of all – nobody had any information about the kinds of deception the 23rd had in mind – they were received with blank stares all around.

One ray of sunshine broke through for Lt-Colonel Simenson. General Omar Bradley's 12th Army deception group was headed up by Colonel Billy Harris, West Point Class of 1933. Harris knew Simenson from the West Point Class of 1934. He felt that he and British Colonel Strangeways should let Simenson and the 23rd in on German intelligence procedures, if only to keep the 23rd from blundering about in the field and upset running operations.

After being let in on the highly classified information, Simenson, to his regret, was then offered a combat command. However, his knowledge of that classified Anglo-American deception material forced him to turn it down. He had to remain with the 23rd which was leaving for France after D-Day as a non-combat unit; he would be less subject to capture and interrogation.

Knowledge of German intelligence methods had fallen into the British hands during the Africa campaign. The Afrika Korps 621 Radio Intercept Company commanded by Captain Alfred Seebohm had been overrun by the British and captured intact. This gift gave British intelligence a leg up on just how good the German information monitoring and gathering procedures were. The Radio Reconnaissance Battalion 13 located in Vitre, Brittany was responsible for listening to radio transmissions in England. Also discovered was a copy of a handbook that contained accurate lists of British units and their locations. It seemed the Germans were tracing movements of these units by radio-direction-finding their broadcast transmissions across the map. The Germans studied those transmissions for frequency of sending and the number and various types of messages. From those early days, most battle units now kept radio silence when on the move.

Another piece of information of value the 23rd learnt was the existence of a German organization responsible for sending trained observers through the lines in civilian clothes – "line crossers" – to report on American, or British unit identifications and weapons inventory. Often, these agents were left behind following a German retreat and were actually local villagers. Considering the top-secret nature of the 23rd's existence (not for nothing was it nicknamed the "Ghost Army"), this knowledge strengthened the need for tight battlefield security and accuracy in mimicking combat units' appearances on the road or in bivouac – and keeping nosy locals away from the rubber tanks and guns.

Meanwhile, the 23rd enjoyed a pampered existence aboard the *Gibbins,* which was surrounded by a large convoy. Occasional depth-charge attacks by fussy destroyers against real or imagined U-boats caused soldiers to look up from their poker hand, peer into the night during deck-side movie projections or pause in laughter for one of the improvised deck shows created by First Sergeant Jerry Gluckin. These shows, with their ribald takes on military life and love usually sent the chaplain retreating to his quarters.

After thirteen days at sea, the *Gibbins* sailed up the Bristol Channel on 15 May, just in time for German bombers to attack Bristol, though the 23rd survived without casualties. Waiting at the dock was Colonel Reeder who informed the unit that their bivouac area was located at Statford-upon-Avon, deep in Shakespeare country. A seven-hour train ride on the London, Midland & Scottish Railway brought them to the "big house" – a vast, rambling Victorian chateau called Walton Hall which belonged to Lady Mordaunt, who lived in a closed-off wing. Nissan huts (slope-roofed prefabricated structures called Quonset huts in the States) located on manicured green lawns and in hand-trimmed forests bordering a swan lake were the 23rd's quarters. To the Ghost Army's soldiers, the big house (which was HQ and officer country) was "the Castle," while its inmates referred to the great pile as "Mouldy Manor".

"We stayed in tents," Bluestein remembers, "... the important people stayed in a castle there. It wasn't really a camp, just called Walton Hall. We practised our manoeuvres, assembling and disassembling rubber tanks and artillery decoys. We had to be able to do it really fast and good."

When not knee-deep in neoprene rubber, some of the men headed off for the Shakespeare Memorial Theatre to enjoy the

Real or fake? Three inflatable Sherman tanks in a thicket of trees, with a dummy 3-ton lorry in the middle. From a distance, they look very convincing. Civilians were kept well away from deception sites.

Bard's repertoire of ancient warfare and lusty humour. Others preferred slipping off to Leamington Spa to indulge in pub crawling, downing warm beer and jollying warmer young ladies who were "… unbelievably friendly" to the young GIs. Local British Tommies on leave referred to the American onslaught as being "… over paid, over sexed and over here".

Bernie Bluestein was one of the exceptions. He admits to being pretty much introverted, a quiet guy. He spent his days sketching, writing letters and keeping a diary of letters sent and received.

Once ensconced in these posh digs, supply became the big priority.

As their equipment was scattered in warehouses throughout southern England, fleets of lorries were dispatched. Technical and electronic equipment was a key priority and soon the specially mounted radios were being installed. The camouflage engineers, meanwhile, had to look to their various decoys to patch and repair after going through some rough handling. One party of five was invited to Ramsgate and an inspection tour of the British army's own dummy equipment.

To consolidate their training, 40 per cent of this 23rd decided to create a formal exercise in three parts, dubbed CABBAGE, CHEESE and SPAM in an area near Thetford about 110 miles (175 kilometres) from Walton Hall between 29 May and 3 June. Neither radio nor sonic effects were figured into this practice exercise. CABBAGE was tasked with simulating an armoured division HQ and its three combat commands. Daylight recon of the area was permitted, followed by a night installation of the dummy armour, HQ, supply, crew tents and other structures combined with camouflage techniques. Requested aerial reconnaissance buzzed CABBAGE at noon the next day to check the simulated armoured division.

CHEESE followed CABBAGE from 31 May to 1 June with another armoured division simulation but with added elements, and SPAM came up last with a "notional" infantry division, regiments of that division, an attached artillery unit and special troops. While these three installations were apparently satisfactory, two new terms were introduced to the 23rd that would follow them to France. These were "notional" – existing only in the mind, or imagination – and the portable GI meal, the "K-ration". Some, indeed, considered the K-ration existed as a meal only in the imagination.

Though no radio communications were included in the exercises, a number of officers in the signal units toured American field units to see what a field radio hook-up looked like and how the combat operators worked. Lessons learned about the process of setting up radio nets between units proved invaluable to the 23rd signal communicators. Above battalion level, Morse was preferred and each code operator had a unique dot-dash sending style at the key. In order to mimic a unit the 23rd was replacing, that style (or "fist") had to be copied exactly. This imitation required long hours of listening and practising.[57]

Apparent satisfaction with the exercises led to the decision to take that 40 per cent of the 23rd across the Channel to France as an advance task force named ELEPHANT.

For Bernie Bluestein, there was a day in England that started out unlike the others:

"One morning I was sitting under a tree, it was early in the morning and all of a sudden I heard a noise – a faint buzzing sound in the distance. The sound became louder and louder and I looked up toward where it was coming from. The whole sky filled with all kinds of planes – bombers and fighter planes. I was just amazed; here was this mass of planes coming over; deafening almost. I said to myself, 'This has got to be it.' That was D-Day."[58]

CHAPTER 15

THE ELEPHANT IN THE ROOM

To deposit the entire Ghost Army onto French soil following D-Day required two months, two planes and nine ships. Naturally, this après-invasion priority was sandwiched into the flow of fighting men, weapons, food and shelter supplies for the desperately battling Allied armies plus the constant back and forth logistics for transporting the thousands of wounded and dead troops between France and England. The 23rd was a 1,100-man non-combatant theory in search of tactical justification, and, as such, a low priority.

The first group across the Channel was led by four sergeants who boarded four LSTs at Plymouth along with the 602nd Engineer Camouflage unit and arrived at 10 a.m. following the landing at Utah beach. Their mission was to establish a fake loading and supply area with "Q-lights" at the night-time beachhead to draw enemy fire away from actual supply landing areas. However, they discovered the beachhead was already ablaze with lights so their tiny contribution would be fruitless. Instead the sergeants went to work with the 602nd Engineer unit camouflaging unlit beach supply dumps. Two of the 23rd were wounded: Staff Sergeant Chester J. Piasecki and Sergeant Tracy P. Black – the Ghost Army's first, but not last casualties.

Next came First Lieutenant Fred E. Fox commanding Operation TROUTFLY – thirteen radio operators from 23rd Signal Company plus three officers and eleven radio operators from the 9th Infantry Division. Using only radio transmissions, they were tasked with simulating the 9th Infantry Division landing behind and in support of the 82nd Airborne. A last-minute change ordered the 82nd to land closer to Utah beach nearer the 4th Infantry Division. This change literally squeezed out the phoney 9th Infantry's radio existence. Fox turned his command into an emergency communication unit for VII Corps and the 82nd Airborne. While they were operating, a rare Luftwaffe visit strafed the rear echelon support area and two more of the 23rd non-combatants were wounded.

On 14 June, First Lieutenant Bernard Mason of the 603rd

Engineer Camouflage Battalion, (Special) landed on the Omaha Beach airstrip with fifteen men and a trailer load of deflated rubber 155mm guns. His command was attached to the VII Corps Artillery from D-Day+9 (nine days after D-Day) to the end of the Cherbourg campaign and the experiment was deemed a success.

Eight days after D-Day, on a cloudy, windy English morning, the 603rd GIs hoisted their equipment onto their backs and marched onto what Bernie claimed was a "garbage scow" for the trip across the English Channel to Normandy. Bernie was the only one without a helmet.

"I did a dumb thing when I was in England and we were in a boat and fooling around. They had barrage balloons with netting on and while I was looking up at them my helmet fell in the water. Then I asked 'Can I get another one?' And they said, 'No, we don't have any spares. But we're gonna be going soon [to Normandy] and if you find a dead soldier, take one off him.' That wasn't for me. I didn't get one till we got to the Normandy assembly area."

For Bernie, the crossing was far from smooth as the boat lurched and bobbed toward its destination. His stomach churned. He stared at water one minute, and then sky as the boat lifted, and then water again as the boat descended. A huge caldron filled with hot water stood on the deck. Soldiers set their canned rations down into the water to heat. When they lifted the cans out of the water and opened them up, the contents boiled out of the top.

The 23rd set foot on shore after nightfall and the men then began an hour-long hike to their assembly area. Although not strictly considered an infantryman, Bernie was issued with a 2.37-in bazooka; two others in his team carried ammunition.

"We got to the assembly area and I was pretty tired. A mob of soldiers was already there. They said 'Private Bluestein, everybody's dug a foxhole here because at night the Germans go over, and they don't want to cause any harm, they just want to cause a disturbance. They'll fly around, and we go with our ack-ack and try to shoot them down. There's flak and stuff that comes down so if you want to, dig yourself a foxhole. There's a latrine there. If worse comes to worse, put your tent next to the latrine. Roll yourself into the latrine.' No way in the world would I do that. But that first night I put my bag next to the latrine and I zipped up the bag ok and I put my hands inside over my head and I just prayed."

During the night, Allied 40mm anti-aircraft batteries fired at low-flying Luftwaffe fighter-bombers, showering the air with jagged fragments of steel shrapnel from the exploding shells.

"The next morning, I woke up and found a piece of razor-sharp shrapnel had penetrated my tent and punched into my sleeping bag. It buried itself just short of my foot. One of the many times in my life that God looked after me. I kept that chunk of steel and brought it home."

On D-Day+11, courtesy of the First Army, a recon party flew over to reserve bivouac areas for the 23rd. They also checked out the 2nd and 3rd Armoured Divisions for future 23rd employments.

To fill out the 23rd's ELEPHANT complement, Colonel Reeder set sail for France with 39 officers, a warrant officer and 319 troops on 16 June. At last, military SNAFU (Situation Normal All Fucked Up) struck. Reeder's LST was mis-directed back to England and ended up near Exeter, where his command spent two nights on the green fields of Bishop's Court. From that relative comfort the 23rd was shuttled by lorry to an over-night bivouac in a "shabby camp" in Southampton. Early the next day, they trudged aboard two LSTs (284 and 335) and once again set sail across the Channel. Then, an administrative error caused LST 284 to be cut from the convoy and sent to anchor off the Isle of Wight for a week. This delay proved hardly an arduous trial. Films were shown on the tank deck. Fresh butter and coffee were served at 1 a.m. each night and the on-board phonograph collection boasted a large stack of classical records. The only hint of wartime discomfort was the occasional "buzz bomb" chugging overhead toward a far distant target on English soil.

LST 335 went ashore on Utah Beach on 24 June and the tardy LST 284 with its sated and relaxed 23rd cargo ploughed onto the beach three days later. And yet, the full complement of the 23rd HQ Special Troops – 39 officers, two warrant officers and 563 enlistees – dubbed the "RESIDUE" or, more casually, the "GARBAGE" – remained at Walton Hall until 8 July when they shipped out to Charborough Park and the estate of Admiral Sir Reginald Ernle-Erle-Drax, K.C.B. D.S.O. The Admiral proved to be an excellent host and the RESIDUE enjoyed balmy summer days peering at his deer and playing baseball. The officers were invited to a warm bath and to share Sir Reginald's port.

This summer idyll came to a crashing end, however when "someone" got into the Admiral's sherry supply. The entire RESIDUE was bundled off to a Liberty Ship, the *John S. Mosby* and stuffed into No. 5 Hatch. After a damp, foggy and mostly unpleasant trip in the bare-bones transport ship, the last man of the 23rd reached France on 21 July (D-Day+45). He stepped off onto an equally miserable shuttle vehicle, a makeshift "Rhino" barge. This clunky conveyance was constructed from several connected pontoons and propelled over the choppy surf by outboard engines used to transport heavy equipment and sullen people.

Meanwhile, Private Bluestein and the rest of his headquarters unit in the 603rd Engineers Camouflage Battalion headed for Belgium where they set up shop making signs, posters and silk-screening shoulder patches.

"Silk was attached to the frames. We cut the designs on wax paper and attached the paper to the silk. Patch designs with army insignia often were extremely intricate. We would carefully squeegee the paint over it. Wherever there was an opening in the cutout design, the paint would come through. So, when we lifted it up, the image was on the fake patch. Then we'd go to the next colour."

"HEATER" (the unofficial nick-name of the 3132nd Signal Service Company) arrived in England on 11 June and waited around until 8 August. Following a boring ride aboard LST 1195, the 3132nd traipsed ashore at Utah Beach and finally joined up with the 23rd at Le Fremonde just north of Coutances. At last, Colonel Reeder had his entire "Ghost Army" command on French soil, eager to plunge into Operation ELEPHANT, their first enemy action as a deception unit.

Actually, due to the stringing out of the command's arrival in France, ELEPHANT jumped off with only 37 per cent of the 23rd available: 44 officers and 351 enlistees. The 23rd had been asked to cover the movement of the 2nd Armored Division when it left the reserves to move into the line between the First U. S. and Second British Armies. This was the period of the Allied breakout from the beaches, which ran into the Germans' grim defence among the hedgerows where every field boundary became a deadly trap for American armour and troops.

According to a German field diary, 9–11 June marked a period of disillusionment for the German command. On 8 June, they had still been looking forward to the imminent counter-offensive which was to destroy the Allied beachheads, beginning at Caen. In the succeeding days, these hopes had to be given up, and German Seventh Army concentrated on efforts to bring only enough strength into Normandy to prevent further loss of vital ground. The delays in arrival of these reinforcements caused increasing difficulty and anxiety. By now, Rommel had arrived on the scene, taking command of the 1st SS Panzer Corps. Rommel expressed his conviction that this counter-offensive, when staged, would be successful. The overall commander in France, von Rundstedt, he reported, believed the Allies were about to make a major assault on the Pas-de-Calais coast, which meant delaying any immediate counter-offensive against the Normandy "feint".

The Ghost Army's deception started on 1 July as the 2nd Armored began moving out of the Forest of Cerisy. As each unit got underway, the 23rd had to replace actual vehicles with dummies: tank for tank, truck for truck. Inflating and puffing away, some replacements worked; others were either late arriving, or late in being created.

Bernie was a big man, but he still recalls the heaving and hauling it took to empty a truck of dummy tanks, lorries or artillery pieces: "They were in canvas bags. So, we had to drag them off the truck, throw them on the ground, dig them out of the bag and blow them up with the air compressor. The bags weren't big, but they were heavy and unwieldy. They had nozzle points all over them for inflating different parts."

Replacing radio traffic was hindered because the 3132nd Signal Company had not arrived yet, so only one radio set was available.

A shortage of artists in the ETO group eliminated any shoulder patch replacements; no bumper markings or Command Post Signs were available. The replacements would have to eliminate all unit identification. And then, the real 2nd Armored only moved four miles (six kilometres) before some of its artillery blazed away, having left part of its artillery and infantry in the same line the 23rd now occupied. To compound the lack of liaison, on 3 July, elements of the 3rd Armored Division began crowding into the area where the 23rd was trying to create a phoney 2nd Armored Division (while the real one was pounding away just up the road). Faced with this impossible situation, the 23rd picked up its inflatables and faded away.

ELEPHANT had proved to be a pygmy pachyderm at best. While being of little value to the 2nd Armored Division, the experience exposed a number of flaws in the operating methods of the 23rd – flaws that would be remedied as a matter of urgency.

Lieutenant Fox compiled a bucket list of "must do's" to be dipped into at once and kept available for every upcoming action. Firstly, virtually no one below the High Command knew what the 23rd HQ Troops Special was, why it was in the ETO, or how to use whatever it was supposed to do. The 23rd needed public relations big time – informing combat commands how to take advantage of this deception chameleon in their midst to fool the Germans with unit impersonations, mock divisions, phoney radio traffic, inflatable armour and fake Command Post (CP) assembly areas – all enhanced with costumed stage play for the local population. It was a hard sell without a string of successes to hold up. The 23rd's officers would have to become deception salesmen – with liaison officers pitching and explaining the advantages of deception to any regular army planner. Lieutenant Fox wrote, "If deception was new to the 23rd, its needs, capabilities and limitations were completely unknown to the rest of the army." The only hitch in this PR campaign was that the 23rd and its work was classified TOP SECRET. Officially, they didn't exist.

There had to be close co-ordination with the combat units being covered. A foretaste of what was to come arrived with unloading the bagged inflatable tanks in the 23rd's assembly area close to the 2nd Armored. Returning later to the inflatable tank dump, the 603rd Engineer Camouflage battalion found some of the bagged tanks missing. In the rush to clear out, men of the 2nd Armored had scooped up three of the inflatable tanks. Two were eventually found and returned, but one completely disappeared. What if a German line-crosser or left-behind Nazis in civvies had made off with the 100-pound sack of rubber? The missing tank was never found.

ELEPHANT had been nearly sunk when the 2nd Armored Division moved out with great fanfare emblazoned with shoulder patches, CP signs and bumper stencils in full daylight, leaving ample tank tracks scarring the countryside. All they needed was a 20-piece military band. The 23rd's lack of liaison with the combat division (due to badly drawn up orders) and the lack of a thorough explanation of the importance of a camouflaged, silent pull out at night, blew the deception. Juggling the radio net to suggest the 2nd Armored had only shifted a bit to its left and was still talking to a notional 2nd Infantry officer (planted with the co-operating British 56th Infantry Brigade) kept the deception alive.

German retreats usually meant leaving behind a number of keen-eyed observers in civilian clothes to spy on advancing troops. Allied shoulder patches, bumper and door stencils and CP signs were noted and communicated across the battle line to eager OKW map plotters. An advancing army's order of battle could be quite easily plotted with such information. Here, creative deception, or "spoofing" entered into play.

The 23rd called it "SPECIAL EFFECTS". They used either borrowed combat unit shoulder patches, or copies silk-screened in the field by artists, chalked bumper I.D. symbols and borrowed or hand-lettered Command Post signs in assembly areas. The army was punctilious in its signs to steer battle-weary GIs to the showers, food line and latrines and away from the odd mine field. Unit members with thespian skills were given cover stories to salt their casual banter in company with civilians (whose loose tongues could be relied upon to relay it further). A sergeant could find himself costumed with the silver oak leaves of a lieutenant colonel on his jacket, shined boots and a tie to intimidate and shoo away GIs hunting for buddies in the outfit the 23rd was replacing. This play-acting was in theory a court-martial offence, of course, but was necessary to fool the lethal audience across the battlefield footlights.

In all, 97 rubber Sherman tanks were set up by Lieutenant-Colonel Schroeder's Combat Command Reserve (CCR) detachment portraying the notional 1/67th Armored Regiment, 2/41st Armored Infantry Battalion, 2/67th and 3/67th Armored Regiments. Combat Command B (CCB) under Colonel Mayo played the part of the 14th and 78th Armored Field Artillery Battalions, and had four platoons of 603rd Engineers set to inflating 100 rubber decoys and setting up 97 camouflage nets – all completed between 2:40 p.m. on 1 July and 6 a.m. the next day. Added to this were a fake airstrip complete with decoy artillery-spotter aircraft and dummy anti-aircraft batteries. Captain Mayo assigned seven guards and three radiomen to keep nosy civilians from poking about as the dummies were being

Which is which? A real Sherman tank compared to a neoprene inflatable rubber tank in the field. Rubber tanks needed constant maintenance to plug leaks and prevent drooping gun barrels.

prepared. Even then, one local farmer stumbled on an artillery piece being assembled and applauded, "Encore boom-boom?" He then touched the "gun". Gradually, surprise turned to clarity and with a broad smile he touched his finger to his forehead and said "Ah, boom-boom – ha ha!" In the future, more men would be assigned to guard duty and no decoys would be inflated within 200 yards (180 metres) of a road.

A light rain was falling throughout the set-up and the camoufleurs of the 603rd noticed it puddled on the rubber tanks making the neoprene sag, giving it an unnatural look. A solution was found by cutting small drain holes to eliminate puddles and later reinforcing the holes to keep them from further ripping. Warm sunny days posed another problem, discovered when a decoy artillery-spotter aircraft exploded from the expanding neoprene.[59]

All efforts at inflating dummy tanks and guns were wasted due to the lack of Luftwaffe planes to impress. At this time, the skies belonged to the Allies and anti-aircraft fire around Allied unit compounds was usually brisk. The thinning out of the 23rd's strength, with just 40 per cent of their total strength committed, meant they were limited to the replacement of only parts of the 2nd Armored Division. Advertising of the 23rd's capabilities had to be trimmed back to mimicking one division at a time until the rest of the Ghost Army company arrived in France from their odyssey of transport screw-ups.

These flaws were the subject of a long and specific memo based on Fox's observations and circulated above Colonel Reeder's signature.

CHAPTER 16

LIVING THE LIFE OF A GYPSY COMMAND

All was not woe for the Ghost Army. The 23rd's bivouac laid out near Écrammeville and Rubercy resembled a bucolic picnic ground. The only problem was blazing anti-aircraft fire rippling across the sky like Fourth of July fireworks. Wisely, everyone dug foxholes beneath their pup tents. Though an unnecessary precaution against direct shelling, friendly anti-aircraft fire filled the sky with sharp-edged shrapnel, which rained down with deadly penetration.

Many of the 23rd took advantage of their downtime to stroll back to Utah and Omaha beaches and take in the huge support and supply efforts coming ashore. Others went exploring along the front lines in search of souvenirs – despite warnings of exploding German booby-traps and overlooked snipers. One group, having read in *Stars and Stripes*, the GI newspaper, that the bitterly contested town of St-Lô had been captured, decided to pay a visit. The rattle of machine-gun fire, boom of grenades and zip of bullets suggested the newspaper article had been a bit premature, requiring a headlong flight back to the safety of the 23rd bivouac.

If any good came out of the ELEPHANT experience, it was learning the value of reconnaissance. During any downtime, the components of the 23rd sent out investigative bands of information seekers to combat units in their vicinity. Virtually every corps and division within the 12th Army Group was studied to build up an unequalled library of standard operating procedures regarding radio transmission peculiarities, CP layout, signage and general "atmosphere" to facilitate "special effects" imitation. Shoulder patches were copied, as were bumper stencils on jeeps and lorries. With their expanding catalogue of information, the 23rd planners could mimic personnel in the 12th Army.

Aerial reconnaissance in an L-5 aircraft also noted a lack of activity around camouflaged areas and dummies. To counter this, white cloths hung to represent washing lines, tyre tracks and footpaths leading to simulated kitchen tents and supply dumps added movement. Oil pots lit to put smoke in the air gave off the air of habitation, simulating cooking and rubble burning. Some dummies should be "badly" camouflaged in degrees of sloppiness, with minor mistakes near the front lines and major gaffes closer to the command areas. A badly camouflaged rubber gun looked even more "real" to a Luftwaffe camera. And by all means add anti-aircraft batteries, real and notional to any major encampment.

Visual reconnaissance was used to study the style and camouflage habits of battle-line units as if they were creating a character in a play, scrutinizing every functioning part, quirk, individual placement of defensive and offensive assets, how they sounded and how they smelled. This endless surveillance would allow the Ghost Army to supplant and mirror any outfit in various, constantly-changing terrains. As they learned, the recons spread the gospel of co-ordinated deception throughout the combat commands. By the end of the war, the 23rd HQ Special Troops had crisscrossed the ETO so often that the majority of their jeeps had logged more than 16,000 miles (26,000 kilometres).

There was plenty of time for this reconnaissance during July as the opportunities for deception during the "build-up" of Allied forces were slim. The Ghost Army had to stand down until breakthroughs occurred in the murderous hedgerow country and flooded lowlands. Eventually, punching breaches in the hedgerows and the bridging of streams and rivers allowed the Allied units to move, amid strategic efforts to keep the Germans off balance and retreating back toward the River Rhine. In the meantime, the GIs made the best of rest and relaxation, trading cigarettes, soap and chocolate for laundry service, fresh eggs and other forage with farm women. "Off-limits" towns and nearby units were visited as Military Police were conned by the curiously successful 23rd HQ dodge, "We're hunting for blue paint." No quartermaster or supply dump carried that colour.

The constant search for any form of drinkable alcohol found a handy local market as farmers traded jugs of "fresh" calvados – apple brandy – to the olive-drab artists, intellectuals and country boys away from home, who were not wise in the ways of booze. During World War I, the liqueur had filled vehicles and cigarette lighters as it came "fresh" from stills to the market-place. To be called "brandy", the distilled alcohol had to mature at least two years following six months of fermentation. The local farmers took fast turnover advantage of the Germans and then the Americans as they flowed through town in search of oblivion from the daily horrors of combat.

As they nursed spectacular morning hangovers, the nearby rumble of exploding aerial bombs and heavy artillery warned the ghosts of the 23rd that they would soon be on the road again. And then they were gone.

Thirty-two miles (51 kilometres) down that road, their unmarked convoy passed through "breakout" country, guided by blasted vehicles, bloated cows, shattered trees, scooped out hedgerows and burning heaps of bloody bandages outside makeshift field hospitals. Another orchard became their latest bivouac, formerly tenanted by the Germans, who left behind their foxholes and roses. Nearby, they found the town of Coutances and the sprawl of the 12th Army Group, the 23rd's new home on the Table of Organization. Their TO code-name shifted from ARIZONA to BLARNEY – thought to be a mildly back-handed crack at these mysterious types who always seemed to be hanging around, peering over people's shoulders and making notes.

The 23rd set up shop in front of its Special Services tent. Signal Company (responsible for the 23rd's immediate radio communication needs) set up staff information and monitoring radios for the 12th Army and pushed along appreciated air deliveries of petrol for the 12th Army Group and 4th Armored Division. They also listened in on radio chatter among advancing units and it seemed that Paris would soon be liberated. This good news was amplified by a British NAAFI canteen – one of 7,000 canteens in the ETO manned by 96,000 personnel – that saw to the small, but necessary needs of the fighting men: cigarettes, coffee, doughnuts, sausage rolls, pasties, soft drinks and ... a measured alcohol ration.[60]

CHAPTER 17

YOU'RE IN THE ARMY NOW - DIVISIONS COME CALLING

A week after the Ghost Army set up camp, the next operation dropped into their laps – Operation BRITTANY. It was to be one of their most geographically challenging projects of the war. The 23rd had to divide into four task forces streaming onto the Brittany peninsula to help combat units stop the German Seventh Army from escaping the Falaise pocket.

This "pocket" was formed around the town of Falaise in the Calvados *département*, in which the German Army Group B, Seventh Army and the Fifth Panzer Army were encircled by the Allies. The battle over Falaise, fought from 7–20 August to contain the fleeing Germans, effectively ended the Battle of Normandy with a crushing German defeat. General Eisenhower wrote of the conflict,

"The battlefield at Falaise was unquestionably one of the greatest 'killing fields' of any of the war areas. Forty-eight hours after the closing of the gap I was conducted through it on foot, to encounter scenes that could be described only by Dante. It was literally possible to walk for hundreds of yards at a time, stepping on nothing but dead and decaying flesh."[61]

The story the 23rd leaked to the enemy indicated that the Allies were weakening their forces in front of the Germans to clear the Brittany peninsula before concentrating on a major push into France – expecting the Germans to continue their withdrawal. Unfortunately, the Germans failed to play along and counter-attacked, cutting the American First and Third Armies at Mortain on 7 August – two days before the 23rd went into action.

Each of the Ghost Army's four columns simulated one combat team-size unit from four divisions: 35th, 80th and 90th Infantry Divisions and the 2nd Armored Division. The notional 23rd columns set up near their respective actual divisions and turned west, while the actual fighting divisions kept travelling east. If the German Seventh Army believed the 23rd's plot, the Germans would think the American Third Army was detaching smaller Regimental Combat Teams (RCTs) from four divisions to clean up the Brittany peninsula.

In effect, Operation BRITTANY was being launched into "Indian country", hostile territory only partially cleared of very unfriendly and desperate German troops. Lt-Colonel John W. Mayo commanded the phoney 35th RCT hell bent for Brest, but came up short as the Germans had left behind designated (not officially trained) snipers who varied in skill from annoying to dangerous. He halted at Dinan until he could get an armed escort. The notional 80th column commanded by Captain Oscar M. Seale, also making for Brest, skidded to a halt west of Rennes. Commanding the 90th RCT, Lt-Colonel Edgar W. Schroeder almost got to his destination, Lorient, under indiscriminate sniper fire during a sweaty-palm trip covering 602 miles (969 kilometres). The fake 2nd Armored made it south to Chateaubriant, where they inflated some dummy tanks, set up their radio and were contacted by the FFI – the French Forces of the Interior – who turned over some German prisoners to be transported to the rear. That accomplished, the men of the notional 2nd Armored Regimental Combat Team went swimming in the *Chère* River.

While not being able to use all of the Ghost Army's full arsenal of deceptions – employing only "special effects", such as shoulder patches, CP signs and chalked bumper identifications plus spoofed radio chatter – the visual display was effective. Even if the Germans were not not befuddled, nosy local civilians and wandering GIs from the actual combat units were taken in by the impersonations. At the Third Army CP, where the 23rd's command was set up by two liaison officers, who managed to get through to Brest and Vannes, a spoof radio net was established linking with the approaching notional columns for the benefit of the monitoring Germans. By 19 August, the Ghost Army's part in the Falaise-Argentan battle was over. The remnants of the German Seventh Army were bottled up and no longer existed on the German Table of Organization.

The most frustrating part of the Ghost Army's Top Secret after-action reports was the lack of conclusive evidence that the deceptions actually worked. Unless captured enemy maps, or intercepted radio confirmed actual American combat units located where the 23rd was carrying out their operations, the phantoms often came and went, without any evidence they had been noticed at all.

That next operation began on 20 August and concluded on 27 August. The 23rd's job was to fool the Germans who occupied Brest by adding notional combat units to the American forces already laying siege to the city. The 6th Armored Division had carved its way through the Brest peninsula and then had been withdrawn. They were replaced by the VIII Corps with three divisions: the 2nd, 8th and 29th Infantry Divisions tasked with taking the ancient fortress city. The Allied upper echelons reasoned the Germans had been showing the white flag with regularity and would give up the city without much fight.

They were wrong. The German battle strength had been estimated at 21,000 demoralized infantry, whereas General Bernhard Ramcke had 30,000 battle-hardened troops including his 2nd Paratroop Division. Not only did Brest's coastal artillery menace arriving supply ships, but the Germans had already made one sally from their fort to rescue soldiers captured by the French. More such bold raids could be expected on Allied supply lines.

The Ghost Army divided its deceptive force into three units: X, Y and Z, with their base camp near Lesneven. X played the part of the notional 15th Tank Battalion in the 9th Regiment, 2nd Infantry Division. The notional 69th Tank Battalion was portrayed by Z in the supposed area of the 23rd Regiment, 29th Infantry Division. Both of these deceptions employed actual tanks from the 709th Tank Battalion to bolster their rubber dummies.

Y Force was sent off with Lt-Colonel Mayo commanding two platoons of camoufleurs, nine combat engineers and a wire team to deflect German counter-battery fire. The 37th Field Artillery was positioned 600–800 yards (550–730 metres) behind the 23rd's flash batteries ("Y" Force) which popped in synch with the fire of the

37th's 105mm howitzers, drawing fire away from the real guns. The flash pots, simulating howitzer muzzle blasts consisted of spent 105mm shell casings, each filled with a half-pint (quarter-litre) of black gunpowder and triggered by a remote copper wire. Over three nights, the artillery deception drew 25 rounds of German fire, while the 37th went unscathed. The Germans were using some of their big coastal guns as the craters they produced were six to ten feet (two to three metres) across. On 27 August, Lt-Colonel Mayo's Y unit packed up and returned to their Lesneven bivouac.

The sonic program fared better. It was the first time the Ghost Army had deployed sonic illusions together with "flash" artillery fire deception. On 23, 24 and 25 August, five 3132 sonic half-tracks for each of the two notional tank battalions rolled into position 500 yards (450 metres) from the Germans and mimicked a division of medium tanks approaching. They came on one company at a time at 30 and ten-minute intervals, settling into position ("harbouring") with speed changes, gears shifting, crackling brush and voices of guides waving tanks into individual positions. All the sounds were so realistic that GI infantry within a mile were certain a supporting tank outfit had arrived.

Meanwhile, Company D of the actual 709th Tank Battalion, comprising M3 Stuart light tanks were positioned behind the sonic deception-plotted ridge line. The light tanks blundered forward into the boggy location to which the sonic programs were luring German anti-tank weapons. Virtually all the Stuarts were knocked out by sinking into the swampy mud, or running afoul of anti-tank fire. Poor co-ordination with the combat commands led X to deceive the enemy into fortifying its anti-tank weapons covering the exact ridge over which VIII Corps launched the 709th Tank Battalion. Most of the 709th tanks had been used to plough up the ground with fake tank tread trails. Spoof radio, special effects and sonic filled in the deception.

On the other hand, Colonel Cyrus H. Searcy, VIII Corps Chief-

Not only large vehicles but also artillery was successfully mocked up by the Ghost Army. This shows an inflated dummy 105mm howitzer. The realistic effect was further enhanced by adding electrically triggered flash-bangs that simulated artillery fire.

of-Staff wrote that if there were any flaws in the 23rd's deceptions, they were, for the most part not the deceiver's fault. Muddled liaison with the army chain of command, especially officers in the 12th Army, caused delays. There were misinterpretations and lack of understanding of what the X, Y, and Z groups needed to do their job. Despite this lack of co-ordination, at the end of the siege when the Germans surrendered on 27 September, German General Ramcke said that he had held out "… pretty well against three infantry and one armoured division".

Colonel Searcy concluded his report on the 23rd, "… the work of these deception units is complete, thorough and correct to the smallest detail. It is believed that units of this type are of considerable value to the army." Though laudatory, his remarks failed to acknowledge the risks of using deception, and the need for constant communication between combat leaders and the Ghost Army's planners before and during a deception program. On the night of 24–25 August, the 23rd almost gave away the zero-hour jump-off point of the 29th Infantry Division. A booming sonic program was cancelled just 15 minutes before the attack into an alerted German defence.

While the 23rd group assigned to the siege of Brest was ducking artillery shells and impersonating American combat divisions and battalions in a bid to fool battle-hardened Germans, the rest were bunking down in story-book France, virtually untouched by the violence of war. The 23rd Headquarters established their bivouac in the charming countryside halfway between Laval and Le Mans. Their elitist overseers, the sprawling 12th Army Group was ensconced 30 miles (50 kilometres) away. Torcé en Charnie was the nearest town. Once formally "liberated" by the 23rd, the locals opened their doors, their restaurants, and their hearts to this band of military mountebanks, soldier-thespians and highly intelligent appreciators of French cuisine and the *joie de vivre* of French culture.

Following a celebration ceremony by the 23rd Signal Company (Special) sharp and spit-shined colour guard, a parade of local firemen and shy giggling school children dressed in white presented flowers to the accompaniment of speeches by town worthies. Colonel Reeder let fly a martial speech ending with a rousing *Vive la France!* This was followed by an emotional rendering of *La Marseillaise* by the assembly. Some of the tears shed were doubtless for the changes coming with liberation. It seems that Torcé was in the centre of the region that controlled the lucrative Paris black market in fresh produce. But, for the beaming, liberated locals and the culture-starved members of the 23rd Headquarters Troops Special, the watchword was "Enjoy while you can."

The *Hôtel du Commerce* in nearby Evron was the best place to sample French onion soup with a floating crouton *au gratin* (with cheese) for the first time. The road from Normandy to this place was strewn with lemon powder packets discarded from K-Rations. Here, the awful stuff came into its own when bottles of Cointreau were discovered and combined into "Sidecars" by Major Joseph P. Kelly, bar master: (1/3rd Cointreau, 1/3rd Cognac, 1/3rd lemon juice).

On 25 August 1944 the assembled 23rd and locals celebrated the liberation of Paris and De Gaulle spoke at Le Mans on his way to the City of Light. Wrapped around limitless Sidecars, Franco-American *"Liberté, égalité"* and above all *"fraternité"* brotherhood was stronger than ever.

Following the giant celebration at Torcé, the 23rd was called up to drive straight toward Germany in company with the First Army on the right and the Third Army on the left. Single-handed they would fool the Germans into believing a strong armoured force was converging on the Pas-de-Calais area and the V-1 launch sites to hook up with the Seventh Army coming north from the Mediterranean. Meanwhile, the First and Third Army would continue their steamroller drive toward the heart of the Third Reich. The preparations and responsibilities would be huge. Everybody had to know their part.

Then, the Third Army turned the plot down. Too late a

commitment considering the momentum of the First and Third Armies' drives and the progress with which they were churning through German defences.

So, with their hands in their pockets, the entire 23rd was dumped in fields outside Mauny (near Sens) to contemplate the folly of high command – and to get wind of a large cache of German alcohol in Les Granges only 40 miles (60 kilometres) away. A small convoy of 2 ½-ton trucks was dispatched to collect "fuel". The collection party managed to load about 520 cases – 6,240 bottles – of Cognac "fuel" which was enough to power a jeep over 22,000 miles (35,000 kilometres) if the Cognac had a high enough alcohol content, which seemed to be the case with this particular shipment.

The bivouac became known as "Cognac Hill". The film scheduled for the 23rd's cinema was "The Ghost Breakers" starring Abbot and Costello. Despite repeated showings during the bivouac, through a cognac haze, the film looked different each time it was shown. Just when things couldn't get any better, they did.

CHAPTER 18

PARIS AND CONNING MPS – AND NOSY OFFICERS

The 12th Army Group was moved to Paris and it was critical that the 23rd should remain close to them. The Ghost Army's next bivouac was Saint-Germain. The 23rd HQ Staff and the 406 Engineers dropped their gear in the *Maison d'éducation de la Légion d'Honneur*, a modest palace built by Napoleon for his wife, Josephine. Down the road, the rest of the unit was quartered in *Camp des Loges*, a military base with tennis courts. For the imaginative 23rd HQ Troops, posting Paris off-limits and then on-limits by the army brass had little effect on their coming and going into the City of Light. They were some of the best forgers in the ETO, from shoulder patches to weekend passes.

Paris appeared virtually untouched by the war since the German commander, General Dietrich von Choltitz declared it an open city, disobeying Hitler's orders to raze Paris down to its last smouldering stone. Its untouched and ancient architecture, its tree-lined boulevards, the Seine River snaking beneath antique bridges, and the girls ... They were like a different species from the barefoot, red-cheeked farm girls of the provinces. Fashion *haute couture* had been encouraged by the Germans to keep their Parisienne mistresses fashionably clothed when dining in fine restaurants and al fresco cafés along the Left Bank and the Champs-Élysées. The atmosphere was intoxicating to the GIs who had been living rough in the burned and blasted killing fields of France since their arrival at Normandy. The Parisiennes who had chosen to ply their feminine skills with the occupying Germans were being loaded into trucks with shaved heads and bruised limbs for out-of-town transport by the Resistance and other survivors of the Nazi occupation.

Elsewhere, Operation MARKET GARDEN, Montgomery's Allied airborne and armoured assault deep behind German lines, had failed with a high casualty count. The American First Army (the "Big Red One") was skewered on the Siegfried Line on the German border and Patton's Third Army had halted its drive at the banks of the Moselle River. German resistance was hardening on every front.

The Ghost Army's idyll in and around Paris ended on 14 September as it packed up its bags of tricks and set off for southern Luxembourg and the XX Corps' mud pit west of Metz. A 70-mile (110-kilometre) gap in the siege between two XX Corps divisions and the 90th Infantry had only the 3rd Cavalry Group to fill the hole. The 23rd had been cast as the notional 6th Armored Division to reinforce the 43rd Cavalry Squadron and draw German pressure away from Metz. The real 6th Armored was moving east from Lorient. Combat Command B (CCB) had already reached Nancy. Assuming it had been spotted by the Germans, the 23rd was left to portray the rest of the 6th (CCA and CCR and its headquarters company).

Only half of the 23rd was committed to Operation BETTEMBOURG to play this defensive role. The balance stayed in St-Germain until 20 September and then moved to Verdun. The remains of the 23rd went to work employing four means of deception: sonic, radio, dummies and special effects. They immediately regretted their short staff as the Germans aggressively bought into the ruse.

Ten radios set up in five networks provided fake communication chatter between elements of the imitation 6th Armored Division and engaged combat units. Co-operation from local XX Corps units aided the seamless transition, demonstrating the number of typical transmissions and helping create the illusion that a new armoured force was moving in. Only 25 decoys were unbagged and set up, including eight M4 tanks, two 2 ½-ton trucks and one jeep. During the night, a collection of dummy M7 tracked 105mm howitzers were erected, but taken down during the day. These few dummies were not intended to foil Luftwaffe aerial reconnaissance, which was busy protecting Berlin against day and night Allied bombing, but to keep the inflatables away from close observation by a covey of Nazi ground agents. Battle "line-crossers," German soldiers in civilian dress and collaborating Luxembourgers who were now trapped in their roles of spying for the Third Reich, were very active.

A platoon of light Stuart tanks borrowed from the 43rd Cavalry Squadron were used to supplement the dummies and provide vehicular activity, churning around the countryside in daylight. Eventually, all the dummies were deflated, bagged and stowed away since the risk of discovery by heavy civilian traffic – some taking notes and others taking pictures – put the entire play in jeopardy. Special effects would have to carry the visual load.

The 3132 Sonic group filled the moonless black nights with the sounds of tank columns churning about, grumbling, clanking, harbouring into aggressive positions for defending the line. Each programme played for 20 minutes, separated by 10-minute intervals. During the day, the sonic half-tracks, with their "heater" speakers concealed, rolled through town adding to the illusion of an armoured division in residence. All vehicles were stencilled, chalked, or whitewashed with 6th Armored identification marks, driven by soldiers wearing the appropriate 6th Armored shoulder patches, and were directed through intersections by military police in 6th Armored helmets and armbands. Even a few of the leather, football-style helmets issued to tank crews were added to the mix and paraded through in full view of the locals.

Sixth Armored Signage appeared at water collection points, bivouac areas and unit CPs. Fires were lighted in the bivouac areas and tents were raised. To populate Bettembourg and the surrounding countryside with an authentic martial atmosphere, a third of the men assigned to the 23rd CCR were cast as genuine 6th Armored Division troopers and schooled in the history of that unit, the identities and foibles of its various commanding officers. They then descended upon the bars, shops and church, anywhere civilians and GIs gathered in amicable conversation. They supplemented and kept an eye on the rest of the 23rd who – usually against orders – ambled into town to take advantage of Luxembourg's beer supply and generally affable attitude toward those who had liberated them from the heavy hand and casual brutality of the German occupation.

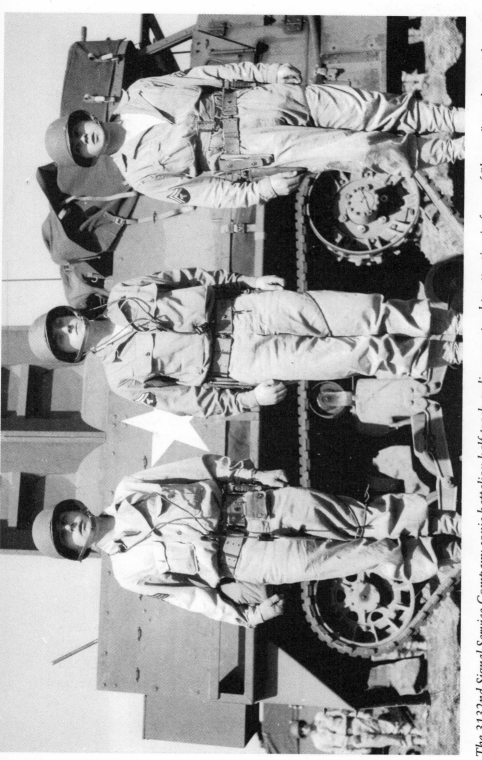

The 3132nd Signal Service Company sonic battalion half-track audio crew stand to attention in front of "heater" speakers with a range of 15 miles (24 km) for sonic deception. Half-tracks such as these were mined with an explosive charge to prevent capture.

This ruse within a ruse soon reported civilians with unusual interest in counting vehicles, jotting down bumper markings and possessing an unusual knowledge of the 6th Armored Division's departure from Lorient and the identities of some of the division's commanders.

To compound the nerves of the 23rd's commanders, while their role at Bettembourg had been scheduled to last only 60 hours, the slow progress of the 83rd Division, as it ground its way through heavy German resistance to replace the 23rd meant their stay had been extended. The Ghost Army would have to remain on point until relieved.

Security was immediately increased. The 3rd Cavalry's light tanks and two borrowed assault gun troops were put to serious work. There was no more play acting. A machine-gun post went up at the watering point and regular armed patrols were sent out from the Combat Engineers. Captain Rebh armed his trucks with machine guns and sent out mobile patrols along the front lines in view of the Germans.

Word came in that the 23rd's relief was definitely due in two days. As this alert posture continued, troops of the CCR began packing up and moving out at ten-minute intervals. Twelve dummy M4 tanks were erected and then "played in" as three armoured units at night. The following night, they were "played out" again to cover the CCR evacuation. All this time, the 23rd maintained their illusion, knowing that at any moment they could be discovered.

As if their nerves were not sufficiently on edge, as the end of the operation drew near and the planners were getting out of town, a jeep full of actual 6th Armored Division officers drove into town following the fake signs and rolled to a stop at the bivouac area. An understanding faux major general told the visitors they had blundered into a "top-secret operation" and pointed them back on down the road.

The illusion had played from 17 to 22 September, a complex operation in six stages carried out under noses of battle-tough

Germans to their front and nosy German spies in their midst. Results of the deception were rated highly. German patrols had increased exponentially, responding to the faux armoured division threatening their front. The German 36 Infantry Division had moved into position opposite the 23rd's sonic, dummy and special effects performance. The Germans had been prevented from capitalizing on an undermanned section of the siege around Metz; and even if they had not considered a counter-attack to lift the siege, they also were fooled into missing the opportunity. And finally, following Operation BETTEMBOURG, the German nickname for the 6th Armored Division was the "Phantom Division".[62]

CHAPTER 19

IN AND OUT OF LUXEMBOURG CITY – DUCKING SHELLS AND NURSING HANGOVERS

On 25 September, the entire Ghost Army gathered in Luxembourg City. The quarters were excellent for the 23rd HQ officers, who were billeted in the Italian Legation building after they were ranked out of the more spacious German Legation by Bradley's 12th Army Group HQ crowd. The Italian quarters were less roomy, but the officers and staff drank from crystal wine goblets and ate meals off gilt-edge china prepared by Madame Nestgen, an excellent cook. The fireplaces were tended by a hired fireman and two upstairs maids performed domestic duties. The headquarters company and the 3132nd took over the Hollerich School while the 603rd Engineers and Signal Company bunked in the *Priester Seminary* whose walls had been defiled by truly ugly German murals.

Bluestein recalled: "The Germans were there before us and it was full of bedbugs. We had to clean it out. The Luxembourg people were very friendly. One thing that astounded me was the fact that the people were located between the Germans and the Allies and also what they had on their walls was interesting: they had beautiful landscape paintings and if you turn the picture over on the other side there was a picture of Hitler and swastikas and depending on whoever was going through they'd turn the picture around."[63]

The Luxembourgers had every reason for the rotating paintings. Their country had been overrun and incorporated into the Third Reich in one day back in 1940. It was renamed Gau Moselland, and 10,000 of its young men were conscripted into the Wehrmacht. Street names had been changed – the *Avenue de la Liberté* became *Adolf-Hitler-Strasse*. By the time of its liberation by the U.S., the population had been thoroughly "Germanized".[64]

For all the comfort beneath solid Luxembourg roofs, all forward momentum had been lost. It seemed as if the 23rd would be having a long rest over the winter.

However, a week later, the front had been reshuffled, with its striking power shifted north. The 5th Armored Division, the liberators of Luxembourg, were being shunted 60 miles (95

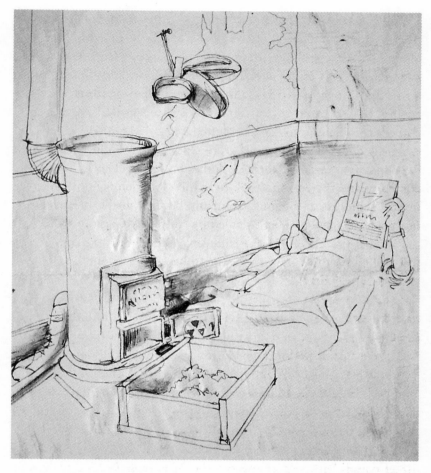

Taken from Bernie Bluestein's wartime sketchbook, this drawing depicts Bernie's billet in Luxembourg – the basic necessities for living.

kilometres) north to the area around Malmedy in Belgium. The 23rd was called upon to "cover" this entire division and help it move undetected in Operation WILTZ from 4 to 10 October. Their task was to convince the German G-2 that the 5th Armored was still in and around Luxembourg City.

This deception depended on the 5th Armored magically disappearing, by moving stealthily at night from Luxembourg with all unit identity markings removed or blacked out from their troops and vehicles – so the 23rd could in turn infiltrate their disappearing footprint. There were not enough extra 5th Armored shoulder patches to sew on 23rd jackets, so the 603rd Special Effects Section was called in to silk screen about 350 exact copies of the patch.

Bernie Bluestein describes the rough-and-ready silk screen technique adopted by the 603rd artists in the battlefield.

"We had the frames with the silk on it. But the problem was how do you get the image on there? We had to physically block out the areas we were going to screen. We used wax paper. We cut out the design by hand; some of them were pretty intricate. We put it carefully on the screen and carefully squeegeed over it. The wax paper was underneath the screen; then when you squeegee the paint on it, the wax paper was in between the outer part of the screen that didn't have any paint – and the paint. It acted like an adhesive and held the wax paper down. So, when you lifted it up part of the design was attached. And then you went on to the next colour."[65]

Red and yellow aerial recognition markers were also in short supply. Nobody wanted to risk driving down roads near "Indian country" and risk getting strafed by their own aircraft. So, the available markers were cut in half.

The radio portion worked smoothly as Signal Company provided 17 radios, gradually replacing the 5th's network two days before the actual move. The Signal Company operators had time to learn to mimic the 5th's radio style and message discipline, allowing the communication spoof to proceed smoothly.

However, while the 5th managed to blot out all bumper markings on vehicles, shoulder patches were still visible on the troops for any German collaborator to jot down. As the sun rose behind rain-heavy clouds, much of the 5th Armored Division's tank and vehicle convoy was still clanking and growling along the main road through churning October mud – shades of Operation ELEPHANT – dooming the original deception plan.

So, being flexible, the 23rd shortened the 5th Armored's simulated move to just down the road and set up their CP's near Wiltz, Luxembourg, about 35 miles (56 kilometres) "less north" than the actual 5th. Improvising, Lt-Colonel Simenson moved out from Luxembourg City on 4 October with 13 officers and 247 enlisted men. Twelve jeeps, twenty half-ton lorries, twenty-one "Deuce-and-a-half" lorries and nine half-tracks kept closed up on the road. To add to the "armoured outfit on the move" atmosphere, two tank platoons from the 5th Armored joined the column with four M4 Shermans and five light Stuarts. The Germans were supposed to think the convoy motored just a short distance and then settled at the edge of a wood, which provided cover for the rest of the force that wasn't there. The 3132nd Sonic added their various programmes of tanks rumbling around, bridge-building and general camp sounds while Special Effects supplied 5th Armored signage and highly visible MPs. CP and bivouac tents were pitched, smoky fires were lit and the real tanks busied themselves churning up the landscape with tread trails. The realistic effects drew in real 5th Armored soldiers who wandered into the bivouac filled with unfamiliar faces and were conned into believing this was a "... replacement unit ready to move, because the 5th Armored down the road was expected to be wiped out". Fake officers sporting polished brass politely shooed the bewildered troops away.

Having ducked that bullet, when Operation WILTZ ended, most of the 23rd headed back to their billets in Luxembourg City. A 3132nd sonic task force headed north for an adventure called Operation VASELINE, which lived up to its slippery title. The sonic force was to be supported by a company of medium tanks, a battery of armoured artillery and a company of armoured infantry, because of anticipated heavy German artillery fire. The sonic program was slated to raise its loud and furious curtain of sound for one night,

Bernie Bluestein in field kit, photographed in 1944 in Luxembourg where the 23rd was based in the months after D-Day.

with the 5th Armored jumping off the next morning. The aptly named VASELINE slid for a number of days and was finally capped for good when the 5th Armored found work elsewhere.

The disappointment from WILTZ and VASELINE irked, but eventually faded away as the creature comforts provided by the amiable Luxembourgers salved the Ghost Army's creative wounds. For three weeks, most of the 23rd's mountebanks, grifters, artists and amateur thespians embraced the city's conviviality, noticing, with time, that the local girls seemed to become less "rural" and more "charming". The arrival of General Bradley's EAGLE TAC 12th Army Group forward Command Post unfairly tipped the social register and dating ratio. General Bradley's arrival also triggered volleys of giant German railroad-gun shells to drop on the city, demolishing swaths of the city's architecture and sadly, causing high numbers of civilian casualties.

CHAPTER 20

ELSENBORN, ILLUSION ON THE ROER RIVER

As the enjoyment of Luxembourg City became more challenging – and deadly – a new assignment came down to move the Ghost Army out to the Roer River, east of Aachen. This new "cover job" was supposed to make life easier for the 4th Infantry Division in seizing control of the river. While this sounded straightforward and routine, it required considerable dexterity in shuffling around divisions. The weather had turned extremely sour, with pelting rain and sleet turning roads into rivers of mud, making rapid movement extremely difficult. Leaning into the downpour draped in dripping rain ponchos, the GI ground-pounders became mud-pounders, approaching the towering ranks of fir trees and tangled branches guarding a dark interior targeted by every nearby German artillery battery.

Operation ELSENBORN (3 to 12 November) revolved around the 28th Infantry leaving the Elsenborn Barracks to relieve the 9th infantry for the grim push toward the Roer River. The 9th Infantry dropped its packs at the Elsenborn Barracks for some deserved rest and relaxation (sleep, a hot meal and a shower). When the 9th was considered rested and relaxed, it was scheduled to relieve the 4th Infantry and move into the grinder in the Hürtgen Forest, backing up the 28th's brutal drive to the north-east.

The forest covered about 50 square miles (130 square kilometres) along the German-Belgian border. Its boundaries touched three cities: Aachen, Monschau and Düren, with fir trees rising to 30 metres (100 feet) tall that blocked out the sun, turning day into false night. Their lower branches overlapped, giving the impression of underbrush to foul up walking and forcing troops to stoop and swat the needled branches from their dripping helmets.

When German artillery fire began, the shells were timed to explode high in the branches. Their explosions rained down hot shrapnel and sharp splinters. Ranks, crowded with replacements, dived for the ground, just as they had been trained. Veterans of forest-fighting hugged trees, letting their steel helmets absorb the plummeting punishment. Replacement casualties began to rise.

Control of the offensive was divided between Elsenborn under V Corps and the Roer River under VII Corps. Thrown into this complex mix, the 23rd had to slip into the Elsenborn rest camp and cover the 4th Infantry's exit to support the 28th chopping through the Hürtgen. Key to this attack was the Allied High Command's lack of direct knowledge of the forest terrain as they sent out orders from well behind the lines. Confident of numerical superiority with a constant flow of replacements and believing the Germans were a fading force, the generals – and even battalion commanders – failed to go to the front to assess actual battle conditions. Reminiscent of the First World War, with a choice of going for the Roer River dams, which could be opened at any time by the Germans, sending the river over its banks, or clearing the "fading force" – the Germans from the Hürtgen Forest – the Allied commanders chose to clear the forest.

The 23rd was involved in two other jobs, so only a third of the command was available for ELSENBORN. Fortunately, only Signal and Special Effects were involved. Using the same tactics that had worked in WILTZ, the 23rd's Signal radios began infiltration into the 4th's radio net while that unit was still involved in combat at the front. For a week, Signal's radios were assimilated into the net until they had totally succeeded in mimicking the 4th's network.

While the 9th Infantry was enjoying the Elsenborn rest camp, the 23rd prodded V Corps to suggest the 9th take a three-day radio exercise. This test allowed the 23rd, cast as the phoney 4th, to take the same exercise which German Intelligence had spotted as belonging to the 4th Infantry Division. One hundred operators and 22 transmitters were employed in this deception. Out on the road, 4th Infantry signs pointed the way to bivouacs, CPs and other vital utilities, while vehicles slopped around in the first snow of 1944. The vehicles sported 4th Infantry bumper markers driven by GIs wearing 4th infantry shoulder patches. Officers of the real division blundered into the fake 4th and stared around at unfamiliar faces until sent on their way by friendly MPs with the forbidding "Top Secret Project" warning.

This time, unlike the 5th Armored in Operation WILTZ, when the 4th Infantry left, they blacked out all their identification and set out along secondary roads in the dead of night. When those troops of the combat 4th Infantry Division suddenly arrived in the shattered Hürtgen Forest, the Germans were completely dumbfounded. A German map overlay captured in the battle still showed the 4th (which was now hammering the enemy) as still relaxing quietly in the camp called Elsenborn.

It took 90 days to defeat the Germans in the Hürtgen Forest but it cost 24,000 battle casualties plus 9,000 lost to trench foot, disease and exhaustion. Once won, the forest was worthless, with the up-river dams still in German hands, which they might open at any time. The 23rd could only deceive the Germans so much – and save some American lives with their surprise appearances – but the Germans rebounded with fanatical zeal spurred on by Hitler's command to "fight until the last bullet".

While deception Operation ELSENBORN was messing with German minds by conjuring up a fake 4th Infantry Division, another piece of the 23rd was enmeshed with General Patton's Third Army from 4 to 9 November. Operation CASANOVA involved supporting a fake Moselle river crossing demonstration near Uckange. The 3132nd Sonic's bridge building-program was warmed up, and providing a devious twist, a diversionary river crossing with a battalion of soldiers from the 95th Infantry costumed as soldiers from the 90th. While this ruse held the German's interest, 11 miles (18 kilometres), down the Moselle the actual 90th Infantry, backed by the 10th Armored Division, launched an attack.

Lt-Colonel Simenson commanded 15 officers, 265 enlisted men and 64 vehicles. The 3132nd Sonic took up 42 of those vehicles, all roped into an area near the Moselle river bank under direct German observation and mortar fire.

Just before the CASANOVA river crossing operation got underway on 8 November, General Twaddle, the commanding officer of the 95th, cut the 3132nd Sonic's bridge-building and armoured vehicle programs, deciding instead to build an actual bridge across the Moselle. The Ghost Army had to settle for special effects' vehicle-marking, shoulder patches and using signage to create an atmosphere that screamed "Here we are, the 90th Division!" However meagre the scam, the Germans bought it. The attack of the combat 90th Division and the 10th Armored near Thionville, 11 miles (18 kilometres) downriver came as a surprise. General Twaddle's bridge attack came to nothing, but there were additional casualties when a bridge recon party of engineers got pinned down on the opposite bank by an alert German patrol, which was reinforced and then the river began to rise. Some engineers did mount a successful deception without the help of the 23rd. They ran outboard motors loud enough upriver to divert the German defenders' interest away from the 95th's successful second crossing. In all, CASANOVA was mostly a flop for the Ghost Army as their control of the situation was minimized.

This loss of control over a planned *and requested* deception was emphasized in a memo by Lt-Colonel Simenson and Captain Rebh of the 3132nd Sonic stressing the points that had gone wrong due to lack of understanding of the role deception had been prepared to play. It was offered to Colonel Reeder for signature and submission up the chain of command. Reeder approved it and suggested a higher-ranking officer leading the 23rd HQ Troops would have had a more effective impact in countering the proposed changes that defeated the deception. Reeder's suggestion was a roundabout reference to getting himself a Brigadier General's star, which he had long coveted, and which could eventually be his ticket to commanding troops in actual rather than notional battle.

The long hold-out German Metz fortresses would stymie Patton's forces as the rear-echelon generals fed in force after force, smashing against artillery-proof casements and internal concrete tunnels, sending battle-savvy SS troops to battlements and into pillboxes. Even the Germans were stunned – and delighted – at the Americans' casual commitment of thousands of troops literally smashing impotently against the forts' steel doors with point-blank heavy artillery, while hundreds of them fell victim to MG 42 machine-gun fire from the stone battlements. The tactics resembled those of First World War trench warfare.

The third part of the 23rd's effort was aimed at the Metz siege and named Operation DALLAS, which mixed a dozen dummy artillery and muzzle flashes in with actual artillery batteries from 2 to 10 November. Dummy artillery blazed away, swelling the XX Corps batteries which included captured German 88s mixed in with their 12 dummy guns manned by 500 men replacing 2,230 men and 48 guns. The 23rd contributed 195 of those men, 36 dummies and the muzzle flash cans. All fire was synchronized to match fake flash with actual battery muzzle blasts, giving the effect of full artillery battalions. Rain and erosion affected the fusing and trigger remotes, causing some misfires and demanding even more robust flash simulation electronics.

DALLAS was not the kind of deception that could be verified for effect on the enemy, but American GIs near the cannonade were completely hoodwinked according to the 23rd's war diary. When the elements of the Ghost army packed up their trick bags and made their way back to their welcoming home base in and around Luxembourg City, they did not know a month would pass before they would be asked to once again reach into their arsenal of deception.[66]

CHAPTER 21

KOBLENZ AND THE BATTLE OF THE BULGE

Following its hectic zig-zag rush from operation to operation in support of the army's advances against desperate defences thrown up by retreating German forces, the sudden inactivity in Luxembourg City sent the Ghost Army into deadly dormancy. After the adrenaline-surging programmes spoofing the enemy, their energy began to fade as they passed the days on this dullest part of the Western Front. Sergeant Berry broke out his 16mm projector and re-opened the BLARNEY Theatre, projecting a variety of films, swapping out reels as new releases became available. By the time his tour was over, he estimated he had projected 2,741,523 feet (835,616 metres) of film to 69,716 soldiers, or about 679 continuous hours in eight different command posts plus a "mobile unit" that could be set up virtually anywhere.

But rather than endure endless thumb-twiddling and garrison make-work duties, the command thought up what came to be called, Operation KOBLENZ, or according to Fred Fox, author of the 23rd's Digest of Operations, "… the most embarrassing operation of the war".

It seems the Germans opposite the Americans, quiet sector across from Luxembourg had been rotating in divisions of *Volksgrenadiers* – untested conscripts fresh from the recruiting camps where they received their rifles, helmets and Nazi pep talks. Facing these German soldiers-in-waiting were rotating American units worn out from the Hürtgen Forest debacle, the Siegfried Line and other combats against stiffening German resistance. In just a few weeks, the 2nd, 8th and 83rd Infantry Divisions were replaced by the 9th Armored, the brand new 106th Infantry, the 28th and the 4th Infantry for a session of Luxembourg hospitality.

Having the Germans use exhausted GI units for combat training sessions for *Volksgrenadier* recruits irked the American High Command. They, in turn, called up the Ghost Army to cobble together an operation that would pin those German trainees in place until 30 December with the threat of a major attack down the Moselle Valley toward the city of Koblenz. The plan would be executed in two phases, the first to begin on 6 December and run until 14 December.

For this deception, the 23rd was placed in a supervisory role to the VIII Corps, providing a medley of deceptions. The VIII Corps drew up a plan to attack down the valley, through Trier to Koblenz, complete with a five-day air bombardment beginning on 9 December. Artillery units under assumed names moved up and increased patrol activity. Doubling down, the VIII Corps followed the 23rd's suggestions and on paper prepared to move up fake ammo dumps and have U.S. agents spread the word among German agents sipping their beers in local guest-houses.

In this plan, the 23rd would provide a notional "division" to the mix. Finding a division that had not already been geographically identified by the Germans was a prickly problem. Finally, the 75th Infantry was chosen because it was just moving into France from England. The 23rd's liaison officer was sent to England to begin "typing" – securing shoulder patches, and other specifications for the Special Effects team – and observing the 75th's operation methods for the switch-over.

Once billeting was arranged by the town mayor, the phoney 75th began settling into their new home north-east of Luxembourg on 9 December. First came a three-day make-over period, as lorry bumper IDs were switched in a hidden vehicle park west of Arlon in Belgium. These vehicles completed the set-up with their usual two-man-sitting-by-the-tailgate "load" of troops, which motored to the notional 75th Infantry's assembly area. All this traffic was duly fed to the Germans via SLIDEX (the weakest American code). At night, the 3132nd Sonic played their "trucks on the move" programme to stretch out the effect.

On 11 December, recon patrols were set out to determine routes for the proposed attack. On 12 December, the engineers began their fake "bridge-building for a river crossing" performance and the next day, real tanks were moved up to buttress the illusion. That night, their number was tripled by the 3132nd Sonic's broadcast of "tanks moving forward and parking". As the tank music played, the phoney 75th Infantry Division began to fade from view. Their spoof radio told the Germans that 75th columns were moving north. Phase one of the ruse had ended with the 23rd heading back in its usual unmarked convoy toward its Luxembourg City home base.

Bernie recalled, "When I was in Luxembourg, the Germans were using buzz bombs, V-1 rockets. I was walking down the street one day, and I heard that darn thing and they said 'As long as you can hear it, everything's okay. As soon as it stops, you're in trouble. That's when it runs out of gas.'

"Yeah, one time when we were sitting in our quarters, and we heard one. We just heard it ... and then it stopped. Boom! That bomb destroyed one of the buildings in downtown Luxembourg."[67]

On Friday 15 December, GIs in northern Luxembourg were entertained by Marlene Dietrich – code-named LEGS bestowed by Patton – singing *"See What the Boys in the Back Room Will Have"* and *"Falling in Love with Love"* after a sensational performance at Bastogne in Belgium. When film director Billy Wilder asked about her rumoured affair with General Eisenhower, she replied, "But Darling, how could it have been Eisenhower? He hasn't been to the front!"

As Marlene sang to the Luxembourg boys, 20 German divisions made their way under strict silence discipline into their assembly area three-miles (five-kilometres) deep on the eastern side of the Ardennes Forest. Their assault, comprising seven panzer divisions, thirteen infantry divisions, 1,000 tanks, 2,000 artillery pieces and assault guns would fall on a front 61 miles (98 kilometres) wide. Gerd Von Runstedt's OKW was loading 80 per cent of their best equipment into this breakout offensive. Hitler gambled that fuel for motorized "Blitzkrieg" armour and gun transport to cover 100 miles (160 kilometres) would be sufficient, and that his armour would capture enough fuel from Allied dumps, to reach the Meuse

River and split the American and British forces. He felt certain the weak and green American forces resting in the VIII Corps area would break before the panzer crush and leave bridges intact and roads undefended – especially the strategically important crossroads at Bastogne. That Friday night's entry in the German war diary proclaimed, "Tomorrow brings a new chapter in the campaign in the West."

On 16 December, three days after the 23rd's departure, all hell broke loose.[68]

Lieutenant-Colonel Simenson, the 23rd's liaison officer, was in Bastogne when the attack crashed down on VIII Corps' front. His "top secret" value was paramount. He and his driver dashed from the city, abandoning his trailer, baggage and four bottles of good cognac.

The official 23rd chronology states, "Organization alerted, documents and records placed in vehicles under guard for immediate departure. Rubber items and special equipment prepared for fire. Guard doubled. Machine gun nests set up for defense of sector surrounding billets. Attacked by air. 23rd gunners posted on roofs fired at enemy planes during entire night." The terse description fails to note the enthusiasm demonstrated by the 23rd gunners as they peppered the sky. It was the first time the largely fake machine guns had been fired at the enemy.

Luxembourg City was not in great danger, but the rush of thousands of fighting reinforcements arriving required another exodus for the top-secret spooks. By the time the Ghost Army was ignominiously racing west, Luxembourg City was hosting four major headquarters: the 12th Army Group TAC, General Patton's Third Army, XII Corps and the 80th Infantry Division, with the 4th Infantry Division only a mile outside of town. Adding to this number was the 23rd Headquarters sticking it out in the former Italian Legation offices to maintain connection to the situation and not abandon their good cook, Madame Nestgen. The brass would communicate via radio with the rest of the unit that was settling into what the 23rd war chronology described as, "… a cold, dirty, flophouse of a barracks in Doncourt near Longuyon, France".

On the way to Doncourt, the 23rd Signal Company was split off to produce another radio spoof – Operation KODAK – to cover the manoeuvres of the 80th Infantry and 4th Armored Division. The 4th and 80th were rolling up from Arlon to join with the 101st Airborne in Bastogne. Twenty-nine radio sets managed to put up a raggedy rendition of the 4th and 80th coding and radio chatter – much of it lost in the tangle of prattle filling the airwaves as the Germans battered their way into the "Bulge" (the salient their advance created projecting towards Bastogne). After 24 hours, the Signal Company shut down.

Christmas was not a jolly holiday. The 603rd had become bogged down in Doncourt and eventually made it to the 23rd's next holiday spa at Verdun, a "dirty and windy French military caserne". The lucky soldiers who had received Christmas parcels chock full of "… plum puddings and Yuletide goodies" discovered their treats had been invaded by rats. Unhappy garrison duty followed: training and guarding the 12th Army Group main bivouac.

The boredom was broken up on 26 December by a small operation, code-named METZ-1, which required 200 Special Effects men to portray a phoney 87th Infantry Division Headquarters in Metz while the real division actually moved up to oppose the Germans along the Bulge. The 3103rd Signal Service Battalion – a sister service of the regular Army Signal Corps that specialized in strategic communications operations – loaned some spoof radio to give the 3103rd tactical experience. Special Effects scattered 87th signs about, posted MPs, sewed on shoulder patches and marked up jeep bumpers to establish the 87th's presence, and completely fooling some GI tourists. The Germans were possibly too busy nosing about for fuel dumps to capture and hunting for intact bridges to care where the 87th infantry brass stored their footlockers.

The New Year arrived at the dreary, cold, unlighted, damp barracks, where no celebratory cheer – neither alcohol, girls nor the nearness of victory – was available. To aggravate the situation, it was rumoured that the Germans were infiltrating commandos into the American lines wearing American uniforms, and speaking passable English. They were causing confusion by changing road signs, protecting bridges from demolition and hunting for fuel depots to keep their armour churning. At any road checkpoint, when a group of new faces turned up, they had to answer a string of American trivia questions. "Who writes the newspaper column, 'My Day?'" (Eleanor Roosevelt) "What's the capital of New York?" (Albany) "How many homers did Babe Ruth hit?" (60).

This was a bad time for the 23rd to be motoring about portraying different units, risking ambush and destruction by their own jumpy troops. One example occurred when Colonel Railey of the American Experimental Station who had helped train the 3132nd Sonic Company was on an inspection tour and was stopped by a 23rd guard post. While the 3132nd knew him well, the 23rd had trained at Camp Forrest and didn't know him at all. They had recently helped stop a spy and were doubly cautious of this stranger with the half-baked story. Railey asked them to call an officer of the 3132nd to vouch for him. The guard asked if he knew Lieutenant Dick Syracuse. Railey replied he knew "Dick" very well. In a few moments, Syracuse approached the guard post and looked Railey up and down. With a grave face, Syracuse declared, "Never seen this guy before in my life." The deadly silence that followed Railey's shocked expression was finally broken by Syracuse's laugh that cleared up the identification.

The New Year brought a return to routine with a cover job called METZ-2. From 6 to 9 January 1945, the 23rd played the role of a veteran Normandy outfit, the 90th Infantry, to allow the unit to leave its stand on the Saar River line east of Thionville to fill Patton's demands for more troops to stop the expanding German Bulge. The

94th Infantry was on the road to replace the 90th at the Saar, but was scrambling to arrive on time. Metz had to remain as the 90th's headquarters until the 94th arrived.

A radio spoof was required to "type" in the 23rd to the 90th network. However, the airwaves were so cluttered, it was doubtful any German radio monitors would even bother with which American division was going anywhere. Panzer commanders were screaming for news of fuel depots and dealing with the *SS-Sturmbannführer* Joachim Peiper cursing "… those damned American engineers!" blowing up bridges as his Tiger tanks arrived.

At 60 tons, the German Tiger was the heaviest tank in the ETO at that time and required stout bridges to support river crossings to bring its 88mm gun into action. Mud, ice, and snow froze between its overlapping and interleaved *Schachtellaufwerk*-pattern road wheels, often jamming them solid. The Tiger's Maybach V-12 engine drank considerable petrol to maintain its slow, 16 mph (26 km/h) cross-country top speed, limiting its 40 mph (64 km/h) cruising speed to good roads. This flaw made them highly vulnerable to Allied air power.[69]

Special Effects slathered the old Metz forts and military areas with 90th signs and did the shoulder patch and bumper marks drill. As soon as the phoney 90th was established, the arriving 94th had to be played in. The huffing and puffing 94th would be relieved by the hard-pressed and exhausted 26th from its place facing the desperately fought-over Bulge.

On their way north from Metz to yet another rapid-fire operation called *L'EGLISE,* the 23rd dropped off a clean-up crew at Briey in France. They were to scrub out an old barracks of the Garde Mobile for the return of the command to bed down until April. The crew discovered the plumbing needed repair and they approached the Briey Water Commissioner. By this time, liberation gratitude had worn a bit thin and the commissioner demanded a *"pourbois"* – a gratuity – for his services: two dozen bars of chocolate, 16 loaves of white bread and a case of soap. Due to the 23rd's reduced field circumstances, the Quartermaster refused. For the duration of their stay, the plumbing remained erratic.

During Operation *L'EGLISE,* the 23rd also extracted the 4th Armored Division from its combat alongside the 101st Airborne in Bastogne so the division could move east of Luxembourg and surprise the Germans. The 23rd would cover this withdrawal masquerading as the fake 4th Armored, brought back to reserve near L'Eglise in Belgium. The security blackout continued for the actual 4th Armored until it arrived at the Rhine. The 23rd kept up their ruse for a few days and then returned to their new base camp at Briey. The officers sought more commodious shelter back at the Italian Legation in Luxembourg.

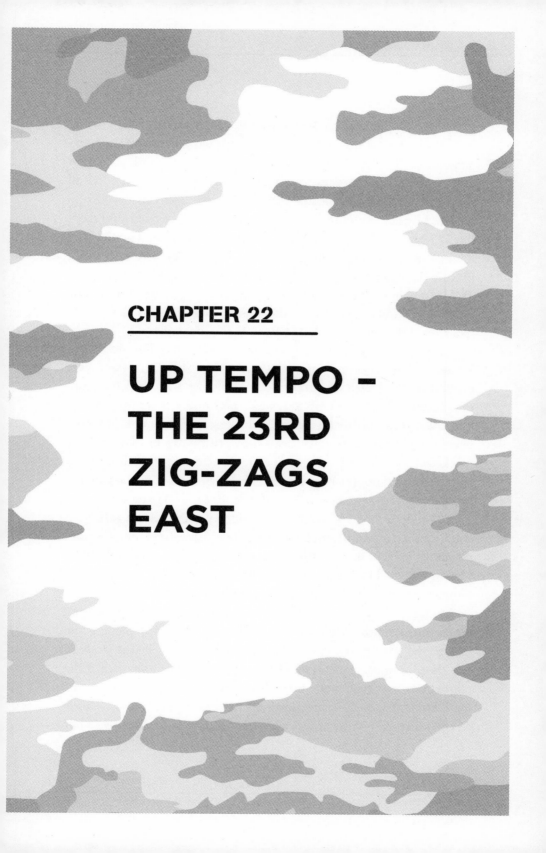

CHAPTER 22

UP TEMPO – THE 23RD ZIG-ZAGS EAST

On 17–18 January, the 3132nd Sonic was called up to the Moselle River east of Luxembourg for a solo two-day operation code-named FLAXWEILER. Once again, they partnered with a combat unit – XII Corps crossing the Moselle River – who provided all the fighting iron and attacking fury. While the 2nd Cavalry Group supplied bridge-building gear, tanks, smoke and stepped up recon, the 3132nd Sonic dashed up and down a skinny road 19 miles (31 kilometres) away and only 500 yards (450 metres) from the river, playing their rousing "HERE COME MORE TANKS!" programme. The Germans responded with a rippling barrage of artillery raining down on cattails, water grass and fleeing frogs. The 3132nd Sonic had tipped their hats and faded away before daylight.

As the 23rd signalmen entered the 4th Infantry Division Mess for some hot food and info on Operation STEINSEL, they were greeted with, "Here come those sons of bitches who helped us into the Hürtgen Forest!" STEINSEL was a radio-only cover job needing only 72 men, four officers and 22 vehicles. The weather had stayed freezing cold over a layer of deep snow, turned to brown slush by truck and troop travel. Spoof radios infiltrated into the 4th Division pegged them in reserve near Luxembourg, while the division actually headed for a surprise visit to Houffalize, north of Bastogne.

While four divisions: the 76th Infantry, 80th, 26th and 95th were dashing about blacked out with shoulder patches and bumper markings removed, the 4th, who did so well in ELSENBORN, reconnoitered Houffalize in full ID regalia. This identification blunder tended to nullify the secret movement of the division.

January wrapped up with a radio deception, indicating replacement of the 95th by the 26th, with the 23rd playing the part of the 95th in reserve. Sadly, the 95th reserve CP was stuck in "… the gloomiest chateau in all Lorraine". Bright moments for the Ghost Army soldiers were: arrival of a bottle of Southern Comfort from home, the weather breaking on 1 February into almost balmy temperatures, and the discovery that heating a chocolate D-bar ration over a pot-belly stove created a satisfying fudgy dessert.

Naturally, these bright moments were fleeting as the 23rd was yanked from its culinary experimentation into Operation WHIPSAW from 1 to 4 February. This time, they broke out the air compressor for dummy work and warmed up the half-track heater speakers to proper sonic pitch, while the Signal Company kept everyone communicating. The sonic part came off well, working with their old partners, the 2nd Cavalry Group to provide enough actual tanks, vehicles and artillery to add verisimilitude to the sonic impression of three arriving tank battalions nosing about in the dark.

German flares lit up the countryside and low-flying aircraft sought out the evasive tanks. A German barrage of preciously hoarded mortar bombs and artillery damaged many trees and shrubs. Meanwhile the dummy artillery, 30 miles (50 kilometres) away near Saarlautern went begging for attention. This excellent representation of two battalions of field artillery drew crickets from the Germans as their aerial recon failed to materialize.

By now, sonic warfare had received rave reviews from the U.S. brass. Operation MERZIG signalled the big time for the half-track heaters as they were pitted against the mysterious 11th Panzer Division. The whereabouts of this collection of German tanks had been reported all over the front, but the strongest rumours pointed to Remich across from the 94th Infantry. In this location, they were fairly harmless and the brass at 12th Army Group wanted them to stay put. Send in the 3132nd Sonic.

This time, it was the 3rd Cavalry Group that provided the deception's tanks and smoke screens, while the Heaters stationed 15 miles (24 kilometres) away near Merzig laid on a virtuoso performance. During nights only, its audience reacted with 138 rounds of mortar fire, 28 rounds of artillery and on-the-hour buzzing by German recon planes and their observers peering down into the dark and smoky landscape pitted with empty craters.

LOCHINVAR, from 1 to 11 March, was supposed to con the

Aerial view of dummy tanks and vehicles parked in the German towns of Anrath and Dülken near the Rhine River. Realistic tread paths were added by bulldozers, and real artillery shells were scattered near fake guns.

Germans into believing the exhausted 94th, posted on the Saar front, was swapping sectors with the 26th. What was actually happening? The 26th was replacing the 94th and its place was being filled by the 65th, fresh from the States with the creases still in their fatigues. The 23rd's job was to costume the 65th into the veteran 94th with some shoulder patches, jeep markings and other Special Effects. Spoof radio would be moved into the 94th's old network to maintain continuity. This shuffle would give the 65th a chance to get some on-line experience under the guise of the 94th playing on the German respect for the veterans of that unit.

Action was heating up for the Ghost Army the closer they moved toward the Rhine River, the symbolic final border blocking entry into the heart of the Third Reich. As the 65th began infiltrating into the 23rd's "94th" position, the Germans took advantage of the unstable situation and attacked. Two of the spoof radio sets were blasted by shell fire. The 94th doubled back and helped stall the German attack. Once the excitement was over the deception con continued: the real 94th moved out, and the fake 94th moved in. The 23rd faded out as the 65th/94th took over.

As the 23rd's *Digest of Operations* says, "The effects of this double-dealing ruse were never revealed, but if the enemy was half as confused as we were, LOCHINVAR was a glorious success."

From LOCHINVAR, the 23rd rushed into a 33-hour deception called BOUZONVILLE, the last for XX Corps. Though it was one of the shortest operations, it led to the loss of two officers, Captain Thomas C. Wells, a promising HQ commandant and Staff Sergeant George C. Peddle, "... an enterprising radio platoon sergeant". They were killed in action on 12 March 1945 near Picard in Germany. The *Digest* noted, "Captain Raynor and Lieutenant Line plus 13 enlisted men of the 603rd were wounded." Medic, Pfc. Jacob Goldberg rushed out into the artillery fire to help the wounded and was awarded the Bronze Star for valour. These were the largest number of casualties suffered in one engagement by the 23rd in the war.

They portrayed the 80th Infantry Division with 23 rubber guns, muzzle flashes and the 3132nd Sonic's programme simulating a battalion of tanks rumbling along the west bank of the river two miles (three kilometres) north of Saarlautern. Special Effects provided the visual clues of the 80th in residence, while the actual division attacked on the morning of 13 March. Again, the results of the 23rd's deception were unknown except for very light resistance to the 80th's attack.

CHAPTER 23

OPERATION VIERSEN – THE VANISHING NINTH ARMY

This story of military deception as it affected the Allied pros-
ecution of warfare from 1940 to 1945 in North Africa, the
Mediterranean and the European Theatre came full circle on the
banks of the Rhine River in the early spring of 1945. All the players
were there. Viscount Bernard Law Montgomery had drawn up his
command, code-named PLUNDER, forged with 1.25 million men,
300,000 tons of supplies and two parachute drops: the U.S. 17th
and the British 6th Airborne. This cast of thousands faced a desperate enemy determined to halt the advance of the Allies at the
last natural defensive line before the Third Reich was laid open to
invasion. George Patton was there with his Spearhead Third Army,
eager to beat Monty's ponderous build-up of forces across to the
German-defended east bank. Added to these stars was Lieutenant
General William H. Simpson's Ninth Army set to cross farther south
from the 21st (in an operation code-named FLASHPOINT).

General George S. Patton's U.S. 5th Division won the race to
cross the Rhine. He did it quietly in boats during the night of 22
March 1945, driving ahead to establish a six-mile (ten-kilometre)
deep bridgehead and capturing 19,000 German troops. Patton's
astonished boss, General Omar Bradley, did not announce the
crossing until 23 March. This was the first crossing of the Rhine
River by boat by an invading army since the Napoleon Bonaparte's
French army in 1795. With the bridgehead established, Patton
crossed over, paused and urinated into the rushing current.[70]

Tailed onto the great Patton/Montgomery/Simpson extravaganza
was the minuscule 23rd Headquarters Special Troops working in
co-ordination with Simpson's Ninth Army FLASHPOINT. Their
deception scheme was code-named Operation EXPLOIT.

This was a deception unit quite different from the straggling
amateurs who traipsed ashore at Normandy days and weeks after
the invasion and began groping their way east with their bags of
tricks. They assumed the identities of combat units, built phantom
bridges, imitated military police and bogus general officers. They

learned to pin German battalions in place with the sounds of ghostly armour and turned liberated – or occupied – villages into stage sets with props, shoulder patches, chalk and dabs of paint on vehicle bumpers. Inflated armour and artillery magically appeared and then, with a hiss of deflation, disappeared back into canvas bags, leaving no trace behind except a few tread and tyre paths leading … nowhere.

It is difficult to imagine the emotions that propelled these secret soldiers from one deception operation to the next: on call, often misunderstood, and inserting themselves chameleon-like into a combat unit's former position under the guns of the enemy. They were essentially non-combatants because of their top-secret classification, and yet they deliberately drew fire from the enemy, cringed beneath German flares floating down in the dark, and crouched in their foxholes as razor-sharp shrapnel punched holes from friendly anti-aircraft air bursts. They succeeded when no one knew they were there, when after-action reports left their names off the typed page.

Describing the 23rd's situation at the Rhine, Bernie shakes his head. "We're essentially sitting across the river from all these Germans … saying 'shoot at us'. We didn't want to get involved with the infantry and that was one of the reasons we joined this outfit. They said we'd be doing camouflage. We assumed it meant painting and netting Army stuff. So now here I am with infantry near the very end, not fighting but asking the Germans to shoot at me. That's right. We're like sitting ducks. We can't go anywhere. We're there for the Germans to shoot at us and bomb us.

"I didn't think much about it at the time, because I knew what we were supposed to do, and I knew what the result had to be. They'd shell us. I don't remember all the shelling. I can only remember when I left the mess tent one morning – about 20 minutes after I left the tent, they hit us."[71]

Now, the Ghost Army troops were at the River Rhine employing

American GIs crossing the Rhine under fire, 23 March 1945. The Rhine River was the final natural barrier before the Allies could cross into Germany, and despite feeling like "sitting ducks", the Ghost Army's deception at the river helped the Ninth Army sustain only 31 casualties.

their skills in Operation VIERSEN (named for a city in the Lower Rhine Valley, north of Cologne), posing as the 30th and 79th Infantry Divisions. Simpson's Ninth Army would cross the river with three corps south of the 21st Army Group. His command consisted of – from north to south – XVI Corps made up of the 35th and 75th Infantry Divisions and the 8th Armored Division; the XIX Corps, comprised of the 29th, 79th and 83rd Infantry Divisions plus the 2nd Armored Division; and the XIII Corps fielding the 30th, 84th and 102nd Infantry Divisions along with the 5th Armored Division. The 30th and 79th Divisions would be shifted over to support the relatively green XVI Corps with an influx of experienced troops.

The Ghost Army would work with the entire Ninth Army to complete the planned deception – an acknowledgement of the accumulated respect earned by the 23rd since its arrival in Normandy. To load the dice in the Ghost Army's favour, Lieutenant-Colonel Merrick H. Truly, one of the 23rd's liaison officers was sent over to the Ninth Army HQ to supervise all of the aspects of VIERSEN as it related to the Ninth's overall EXPLOIT deception.

The Germans had to believe that the Ninth Army would not be able to launch a river crossing attack before 1 April 1945. Genuine concentrations of troops and supplies in the XVI Corps area were to be concealed while a notional attacking force, the 30th and 79th Divisions, would be created in the XIII Corps zone between Düsseldorf and the Erft River. The creation and preparations for this phoney force would be dragged out, pushing the attack date to 1 April, well past PLUNDER's real launch, planned for 24 March.

The enemy would be at the top of its game facing the massive Allied force on the west bank of the Rhine. At their backs was Hitler's "Stand to the last man – last bullet" decree, reinforced by Himmler's draconian orders to shoot any slackers and hang deserters. Their resources had been depleted by their drawn-out retreat, but the Rhine was as symbolic to Germans as the Thames to the British or the Mississippi to the Americans.

Unlike with most of the 23rd's operations, this time the Luftwaffe was a regular visitor to the Rhine's west bank. These were the same high speed Arado AR 234B-2 turbojet bombers and Me 262/U3 recon jet fighters that had whistled through the largest concentration of anti-aircraft weapons on 7 March at the earlier Rhine crossing over the briefly-secured Remagen Bridge. The Americans had counted 367 different German Luftwaffe aircraft attacking the bridge over the 10 days that it withstood bombardment.

On 19 March, the 23rd's Intelligence officer, Captain Joseph P. Kelly, drew up an estimate of German intelligence competencies. It was a long and thorough list. Kelly had no reason to expect less German diligence. Fast recon aircraft with cameras that could outfly any U.S. fighter were the big fear. High speed runs meant no visual observers of the EXPLOIT preparations, just cameras blazing away. German aerial reconnaissance, as FORTITUDE and QUICKSILVER had learned, did not use stereoscopic cameras so their images were "flat" and required sun shadows to reveal terrain and camouflage characteristics. Decoys stood a better chance as stand-ins for the iron and steel Sherman tanks, lorries in car parks and other dummy installations.

On the ground, in the Ninth Army sector alone, more than 35,000 residents had been scoured from their homes to clear assembly areas of nosy German agents in civilian clothes. Telephone lines still existed across the river, making eyeball observations of military value a simple phone call away. For the 23rd, this level of security was routine, but a heavy clampdown on Ninth Army personnel was critical.

Special Effects emptied their full bag of tricks: shoulder patches for all personnel, more than 200 division signs posted, jeep, truck and armour painted with division identification marks.

Bernie recalled, "Yeah, we got involved with stencilling the equipment and making sure we had the right patches on. We were simulating two divisions. We were only 1,100, but we were simulating those 30,000 guys."[72]

All Military Police helmets bore the correct division insignia and all officers being portrayed wore the correct rank, which caused some confusion. Former West Point graduate officers who were senior to Captain Rebh came to visit. They found him wearing the eagles of a full colonel as "commander" of the notional 119th Infantry Regiment. They were stunned by his rapid advancement. Rebh had to play out his role, politely sending them off, returning appropriate salutes. Like the radio show, "Queen for a Day", sergeants became majors and corporals were saluted as lieutenants. Acting talent and quick improvisation were essential.

General Simpson issued the following order concerning EXPLOIT: "This information will be disseminated to the minimum number of subordinate commanders and staff officers to enable adequate implementation of this plan. A list of these individuals will be maintained at each Corps Headquarters."

German radio monitoring was always considered both accurate and relentless in tracking U.S. troop movements. The 23rd Signal Unit's insinuation into the Ninth Army radio network would have to be seamless.

The overall Ninth Army EXPLOIT deception plan as devised by the 23rd's experts was described by (now) Captain Fred Fox in his *Digest of Operations of the 23rd Headquarters Special Troops.*

"XVI Corps: The assault build-up was done under the most absolute security. Divisions – 30th and 79th – coming into the zone moved in darkness and remained visually obliterated (no shoulder patches or Corps/Division markings). Artillery positions and engineer parks were either hidden or camouflaged. Artillery registration (gun targeting shots) was done during battery fire on normal harassing fire missions.

"XIII Corps: The 23rd prepared all evidences for a river crossing operation, the maximum effect to be attained about April 1. Corps Division Artilleries stepped up fire and spread out installations by the addition of rubber dummies from the 23rd. Corps Engineers established new parks and paraded with bridging equipment. Preparations were supplemented by dummy items, installed and maintained by personnel from the 84th Infantry and 604th Engineer Camouflage Battalion. The emplacements were constructed along the front similar in nature and number to XVI Corps. The anti-aircraft artillery was built with sixty-four 40mm and sixteen 90mm rubber guns furnished by the 23rd. On some nights, on small pretexts, the (actual) anti-aircraft sent up fierce demonstrations of firepower which rivaled their activity on the Normandy beaches. Infantry patrolling was intensified to a point 50 per cent greater than that done by the XVI Corps. The (actual) 30th and 79th Divisions, which had transferred to the XVI Corps were notionally assembled in the XIII Corps zone by the 23rd. Two battalions of real infantry – from the 84th and 102nd – were attached to each of the phoney divisions to help fill out the picture.

"XIX Corps: Artillery leaving the corps zone to support the XVI Corps was required to leave positions intact and well camouflaged. Tank destroyer emplacements similar to XVI and XIII corps were installed along the front. The 83rd Infantry Division dropped back to the Maas River area to cover where the 30th and 79th had been undergoing river crossing training.

"The Ninth Army air support given by 29th Tactical Air Command flew reconnaissance over the XIII zone on the same scale as the XVI. Army medical installations gave the impression that the attack would take place in the XIII Corps zone. Only one evacuation hospital was installed in the forward part of the XVI zone. A spoof Army Traffic Control network operated by the 23rd brought attention to the XIII Corps by reporting large vehicular movements in that area.

"The 23rd's notional divisions were brought up and displayed to the east and west of Viersen. All means of deception were employed: sonic, dummies, radio and special effects. Each 'division' had nearly 400 extra rubber vehicles including five dummy liaison aircraft (on

A dummy L-5 reconnaissance aircraft on a dummy landing strip in a field. In Operation VIERSEN – 23rd's final and most dramatic performance in March 1945 – inflated rubber planes were used to fool the Germans into converging to defend a point on the Rhine River miles away from the actual attack. To achieve this, the Ghost Army successfully impersonated two full divisions (30,000 men) – an extraordinary feat.

a makeshift airstrip). Aerial photos of these installations showed a remarkably authentic layout."

To further pin the Germans' defences into preparing for a 1 April crossing, the 23rd divided into two assault divisions – the fake 30th and 79th – on 17 March at the Maas River training centre at Sittard in the Netherlands. While portraying these actual units, both in uniforms, ranks and radio traffic, the 23rd imposters moved into the XIII zone. To fill out the move, the actual 1st Battalion, 334th Infantry Regiment, 84th Infantry Division, and the 430th Antiaircraft Battalion, Batteries C&D, were attached both as security and to create the impression of 13,000 men.

Troops playing the roles of the combat units' officers and communications specialists were schooled in the names and ranks of their actual counterparts to use in all conversations where eavesdroppers could be expected. Laundry was hung out to dry in the bogus bivouacs. Disposing of any rubbish that might contain even fragments of unit information was forbidden.

The 23rd's success in confounding the Germans was rewarded on March 18, when 549 enemy artillery rounds plunged down into a west bank artillery park and blasted dummy guns into shards of smoking rubber. Further interest was also shown by the Luftwaffe, as their flight volume increased with cameras replaced by hammering cannon and machine-gun strafing, punctuated with 250 and 500-pound bombs. Fake bivouacs and dummy supply dumps were decimated.

Bernie Bluestein recalls, "For our last mission at the Rhine River, we had to simulate two Army divisions. Everyone got fake patches and some privates became majors. There were about 300 of us and I learned how to talk like the person I was imitating. We had a sound truck, simulating tanks and trucks for troops that weren't there. Next morning the shells came in and one of my friends got hit by shrapnel. We were responsible for keeping the Germans pinned there; sort of telling them 'Here we are!' For someone who joined the camouflage unit because I didn't want to get shot, I was always ending up in the line of fire."[73]

According to Captain Kelly, Luftwaffe air activity maintained its increase over the XIII Corps zone. Into the night under the blaze of flares, the 23rd's bogus crossing preparations were relentlessly photographed through a hail of anti-aircraft fire and scorching beams of searchlights.

Finally, at midnight on 24 March 1945, Montgomery's massive Operation PLUNDER rolled out, following Lancaster bomber streams overhead and the thunder of artillery. Simpson's Ninth Army crossed at the XVI Corps zone well south of the 23rd's area of operation and fell on the shell-shocked German defenders, sustaining only 31 casualties. The Germans, unprepared and dazed from artillery and aerial bombardment, reeled back and broke under the crushing onslaught, and fell back in full retreat until the 116th Panzer Division arrived to create a new defence line.[74]

Intelligence gleaned following the successful Rhine crossing showed the Germans were completely surprised by the weight of the Ninth Army's attack. A captured map overlay showed the 79th located exactly where the 23rd had portrayed it far from the actual crossing, while the 30th had disappeared altogether. "There is no doubt," the 79th G-2 wrote in the after-action report, "... that Operation Viersen materially assisted in deceiving the enemy with regard to the real dispositions and intentions of this army."

Of course, the 23rd Headquarters Special Troops were not mentioned in that after-action report, because they were still classified Top-Secret. As with all their operation, they packed up their trick bags, heater half-tracks, paint brushes, silk-screening paraphernalia, surviving rubber guns, tanks, airplanes and trucks, and headed back in their ghostly convoy to their headquarters in Briey, France with its dubious plumbing.

CHAPTER 24

THE GHOST ARMY DOES NOT BECOME A PART OF HISTORY

Following the Rhine crossing, the 23rd had accomplished its goal, using deception to help advance the American Armies battling through Germany on their way to the Allied victory. Now that victory was almost won in Europe, and the 23rd was no longer needed there, it appeared likely that they would be shipped to the Pacific Theatre, after a 30-day furlough in the United States.

As it turned out, while waiting for orders, the 23rd actually broke Army rule Number One: "Never volunteer!" They *requested* more assignments with the 12th Army Group, who had no problem accepting their generous offer.

The Army's planners proceeded to redeploy the 23rd into four different roles. The Signal Company acted as a monitoring unit for the corps. The wire platoon was told to recycle "spiral-4" communications wire and managed in five weeks to assemble 800 miles (1,300 kilometres) of wire. At $500 per mile, the American taxpayer was ahead by a grand total of $400,000. Another section of the Signal Company worked in the Twelfth Army Group code room. On 7 May they were first to get the news that Eisenhower had plans to send a number of troops home.

The remaining troops were sent to the Fifteenth Army, which loaned them to the XXIII Corps to handle the sensitive and sometimes dangerous job of organizing 100,000 Displaced Persons – innocent victims of war who were now homeless, hungry and possessed little more than the clothes on their backs. Eisenhower had specified that a DP was *"a civilian outside the national boundaries of his or her country by reason of war who was desirous but unable to return home or find a home without assistance …"*[75]

On 11 April 1945, the 23rd troops took on their new assignment in two capacities: Camp managers and the DP staff section to the XXIII Corps.

One hundred thousand refugees representing 26 nationalities were spread around into five camps in the Saar-Palatinate region in south-western Germany under supervision of the Ghost Army's

406th Combat Engineers, 603rd Engineers and 3132 Sonic: Baumholder (406th); Trier (603rd); Bitburg (603rd); Wittlich (603rd) and Lebach (3132nd). The 23rd Headquarters staff settled into the Hotel Hermes in Idar-Oberstein in the Rhineland area along with the XXIII Corps. Their prize cook, Madame Nestgen was smuggled across the Luxembourg border so that the staff was able to enjoy the same high-quality cuisine they'd had at the Italian Legation.

The army, which was used to handling supplies, moving and billeting troops, found the task of feeding, clothing, housing and refereeing war-weary Europeans a greater challenge. DPs often fought among themselves. Russians and Poles harboured deep-seated resentment against German civilians and these factions often beat, robbed or killed their former enemies. To make matters worse, they could easily unearth leftover weapons half-buried in former battlefields.

One soldier recalled seeing a crowd of Poles moving around shouting and gesturing at a man who was lying on the ground, his head bashed in and a tent pole next to his body. The GI raised his rifle and fired three shots to disperse the crowd and call attention to the situation. MPs arrived and took over. The GI later learned that the Poles had recognized the dead man as an informer for the enemy, so they had lost no time in carrying out their own form of justice.

Challenges existed outside the camps as well. Russians often broke into the homes of German citizens, confiscating food and beating their former enemies. Another time, a GI was ordered to escort a German dairy farmer while he delivered cans of milk. The GI carried a sub-machine gun to ward off any Poles or Russians, who were prone to attack Germans, no matter their occupation.

Bernie's post-Rhine River job was typical. "I was tall so they made me an MP."[76]

And, since no good deed goes unpunished, it was not long before word spread among the DPs outside the camps that the Allies were capable of humane treatment. The camp population gradually increased, meaning that food and facilities had to be constantly stretched to accommodate new arrivals.

Eventually the 23rd HQ Special Troops did manage to group the DPs into thirteen separate camps organized by nationality, thus avoiding any more brutality. With peace maintained, they could now concentrate on the basics, especially when dealing with the refugees from central Europe. About 43,000 were unfamiliar with such modern facilities as flushable latrines.

During this period, virtually all GIs in the ETO had only one nagging thought: "When can I go home, or will they send me to Japan?"

By 28 April, the 23rd was relieved of their DP camp duties, to be replaced by field artillery units attached to the XXIII Corps. The 23rd troops then served in the Corps staff section. The good news came in late May when the Ghost Army received orders to return home. They were sent to the hills outside Idar-Oberstein to make "Preparations for Overseas Movement" (POM). Sadly, they were forced to sleep in tents, something they hadn't experienced since Operation CASANOVA in 1944.

After a three-day journey from Idar-Oberstein, the troops arrived at the staging area at Rouen, in northern France on 16 June. One can only imagine the joy the troops felt as they travelled through the French countryside – it was spring, flowers and crops were in full bloom and the country was finally at peace.

In his report, *Digest of Operations: 23rd Headquarters Special Troops*, Fred Fox wrote: "*... France never looked so beautiful. The wheat was ripe and mixed with poppies and blue-bells. To men dizzy with thoughts of home, every field could have been a rippling flag – or the neon lights of Broadway, a colorful county fair, a mardi-gras [sic], or a whirling rodeo in Flagstaff, Arizona.*"

Along the way, grateful citizens approached, offering wine and champagne, which the troops accepted gladly, not wishing to offend.

As Bernie Bluestein recalled:

"We were in a place where they make champagne. So, the guys all got the champagne and they drank it down. Most of them got sick because it was all green. Then another time we went to a family and I was going to exchange my cigarettes for something, because I didn't smoke. And I didn't drink, but this Frenchman wanted to toast us. They poured us all something strong – most likely Calvados – and I didn't know how to drink that stuff so I just took it and drank it down. Everybody else was sipping it. I thought I would die my throat was so burned."[77]

Still, one last barrier haunted all of them – the complex point system. Soldiers accumulated points based on length of service, marital status, time overseas, decorations, parenthood, age, combat duty, etc. The more points one had, the greater the possibility for discharge. Almost all of the 23rd felt fairly certain that after a celebratory reunion with family and friends in the U. S., they would be shipped to the Pacific. Yet, it was hard to imagine how their deception tactics could be carried out as the Allies fought through a string of islands on their way to the Japanese mainland. They had heard of the Japanese fighting to the death according to the fanatical code of Bushido. Marine, Navy and Army casualties were already horrendous.

Finally, on 23 June 1945 the American Ship *General O. H. Ernst* sailed out of Le Havre bound for Newport News, Virginia with the 23rd Headquarters Special Troops on board. The ETO washed away astern in the ship's frothing wake. On 6 and 9 August 1945, after obtaining the consent of the United Kingdom, as required by the Quebec Agreement, the United States dropped two atomic bombs on the Japanese cities of Hiroshima and Nagasaki, effectively ending World War II and any speculation about a final operation for the men of the Ghost Army, which, of course, didn't exist.

As for Bernie's homecoming, "When I got rotated home, I went to Camp Shelby in Hattiesburg, Mississippi, where I was discharged."[78]

The Ghost Army's deception equipment was recycled to be used in the army's "Aggressor Force" training program. It was a hypothetical enemy to train against, with the unstated goal of fighting communism.

As for the artists, actors, technicians, magicians and designers of the Ghost Army, they kept silent about their war experiences because the records were still classified Top Secret. Some stayed in the military to continue their careers, while most returned to civilian life faced with answering the question, "What did you do in the war, daddy?" They could reply with an ETO travelogue of impressive adventures without ever mentioning how they had a personal hand in conning Adolf Hitler.

THE END

BERNIE BLUESTEIN'S PEACETIME YEARS:

" After the war I went back to the Cleveland School of Art and finished in 1947. I studied to be an industrial designer and worked 15 years for a large industrial design firm in Chicago that no longer exists. I designed products like the early Zenith Television sets. I moved on and went to Sunbeam where I worked 15 years, designing their home products until I retired in 1983. I decided I had never done any fine artwork for myself and wanted to see what it was all about. In 1989, I came to Harper College in Palatine, Illinois and tried every course they had – sculpture, painting and more."

In August 2018, Bernie turned 95 years old. His incredible sculpture is displayed throughout the Harper College campus and featured in magazines and the press. He is now considered Harper's "Student Emeritus".

Encore: Top-secret recognition of the 23rd's contribution to the Rhine Crossing from General William Simpson, 9th Army

(photo of the actual letter sent by Simpson announcing the unit commendation)

HEADQUARTERS
NINTH UNITED STATES ARMY
Office of the Commanding General

APO
29 March 1945

SUBJECT: Commendation

TO : Commanding Officer, 23d Headquarters Special Troops,
Twelfth Army Group.
THRU: Commanding General, Twelfth Army Group

1. 23d Headquarters Special Troops, Twelfth Army Group, was
attached to NINTH UNITED STATES ARMY on 15 March 1945 to partici-
pate in the operation to cross the RHINE River.

2. The unit was engaged in a special project, which was an
important part of the operation. The careful planning, minute
attention to detail, and diligent execution of the tasks to be
accomplished by the personnel of the organization reflect great
credit on this unit.

3. I desire to commend the officers and men of the 23d Headquarters Special Troops, Twelfth Army Group, for their fine work
and to express my appreciation for a job well done.

W. H. Simpson
W. H. SIMPSON,
Lieutenant General, U. S. Army,
Commanding.

SURVIVING MEMBERS OF THE GHOST ARMY AS OF THIS WRITING

Bill Anderson, Bud Bier, Bernie Bluestein, Bill Brown, John Cole, Bill Enoch, Harold Flinn, Les Gates, Nick Leo, Mark Mallardi, Bernie Mason, Bill Maynard, Stanley Nance, Gazo Nemeth, Seymour Nussenbaum, Gil Seltzer, Arthur Shilstone, A.B.Wilson, John Zeutenhorst

(courtesy: Rick Beyer)

EPILOGUE: MONUMENT DEDICATION CEREMONY, LUXEMBOURG CITY TO THE 23RD HQ SPL TROOPS, 2018

On 26 September 2018 in Bettembourg, Luxembourg, Deputy Chief of Mission, Kerri S. Hannan attended the official dedication of a historical marker honouring the Ghost Army.

The historical marker outside Bettembourg, Luxembourg erected to honour the men of the 23rd Headquarters, Special Troops in September 2018 reads:

> *The 23rd Headquarters Special Troops – a top-secret U.S. Army deception unit – used inflatable tanks and artillery, sound effects, radio trickery and impersonation to fool the Germans on the battlefields of Europe during World War II. It was known as "The Ghost Army."*

From September 15-22, 1944, the 23rd staged Operation BETTEMBOURG out of these woods. Roughly 400 GIs successfully posed as 8000 heavily armed troops from the U.S. 6th Armored Division. Using a wide array of deception techniques, they helped hold a dangerously undermanned segment of General George Patton's front line, as the Third Army attacked Metz to the South.

The men of the 23rd carried out 21 major battlefield deceptions during the war, often perilously close to the front lines. Their creative tactics saved countless lives and contributed mightily to Allied victory.

"Rarely, if ever, has there been a group of such a few men which had so great an influence on the outcome of a major military campaign."

Mark Kronman, United States Army analyst

ENDNOTES

1. Stroud, Rick. *The Phantom Army of Alamein: How Operation Bertram and the Camouflage Unit Hoodwinked Rommel.* London: Bloomsbury, 2012

2. Ibid, Stroud, p. 46

3. Barkas, Geoffrey; Barkas, Natalie. *The Camouflage Story (from Aintree to Alamein).* London: Cassell and Company, 1952, pp. 153–163

4. Ibid, Stroud, pp. 124–133

5. Ibid, Stroud, p. 132

6. Ibid, Barkas, p. 196

7. Imperial War Museum, London. *North Africa Campaign Reports on OPERATION BERTRAM, 1943*

8. Atkinson, Rick. *An Army at Dawn: The War in North Africa, 1942–1943.* New York: Henry Holt and Company, 2002, p. 411

Fisher, David. *The War Magician.* New York: Coward-McCann, Inc. 1983 reprint, pp. 275–285

9. Ibid, Atkinson, p. 411

10. *http://www.bbc.co.uk/history/worldwars/wwtwo/ff5_second_alamein.shtml,*

Ibid, Fisher, pp. 292–295

11. Reit, Seymour. *Masquerade—the Amazing Camouflage Deceptions of World War II.* New York: New American Library (Signet imprint), 1976.

12. Levine, Joshua. *Operation Fortitude: The Greatest Hoax of the Second World War.* London: Harper Collins, 2011.

13. Tate, Tim. *Hitler's British Traitors.* London: Icon Books, Ltd., 2018 BBC "World News Update" interview, Dan Damon, September 6, 2018

14. Montagu, Ewen. *The Man Who Never Was.* New York: Scholastic Book Services, 1967, p. 14

15. Macintyre, Ben. *Operation Mincemeat: How a Dead Man and a Bizarre Plan Fooled the Nazis and Assured an Allied Victory.* New York: Harmony Books, 2010

16. Lieutenant Colonel Michael J. Donovan, United States Marine Corps and Colonel (USMC Ret.) Brian D. Moore, Project Advisor. U.S. Army War College, Carlisle Barracks, 17013-5050. 20020806 322 USAWC *Strategy Research Project, Strategic Deception, Operation Fortitude.* p. 139

17. Ibid, Donovan and Moore, Army War College, pp. 140–141

18. *The Oxford Companion to World War II.* Oxford University Press, Oxford, New York, 1995, p. 579

19. Clausewitz, Carl V. *On War.* Edited and translated: Michael Howard, Peter Paret. Princeton, NJ: Princeton University Press, 1976, p. 202

20. Cubbage, T. L. Edited by Michael I. Handel, *Strategic and Operational Deception in the Second World War.* New Jersey: Frank Cass & Co. Ltd, NJ, 1987, pp. 93–107

21. Gawne, Jonathan. *Ghosts of the ETO: American Tactical Deception Units in the European Theater, 1944–1945.* Havertown, PA: Casemate, 2002, pp. 12–15

22. Smith, Constance Babington. *Evidence in Camera.* London: David & Charles, 1957, pp. 107–108

23. Levine, Joshua. *Operation Fortitude: The Story of the Spy Operation that Saved D-Day.* London: Harper Collins UK, 2011

Holt, Thaddeus. *The Deceivers: Allied Military Deception in the Second World War.* New York: Scribners, 2004

24. Fairhead, Huby. *Decoy Sites, Wartime Deception in Norfolk and Suffolk.* Norfolk and Suffolk Aviation Museum.

25. Churchill, Winston. *Grand Alliance.* Boston: Houghton Mifflin Company, 1950, p. 608

26. Ibid, Gerard, pp. 24–25 and Ibid, Gawne, pp. 66–67

27. Dwyer, John B. *Seaborne Deception: The History of U.S. Navy Beach Jumpers*. New York: Praeger Publishers, 1992, pp. 63–75

28. Ibid, Dwyer, p. 75

29. Tooley, Peter J. *Operation Quicksilver*. Romford, Essex: Ian Henry Publications, Ltd., 1988, pp. 9–10.

30. Ibid, pp. 13–14

31. Ibid, p. 21

32. Ibid, pp. 33–35

33. Ibid, pp. 50–64

34. Handel, Michael I. *Strategic and Operational Deception in the Second World War*. London: Frank Cass, 1989, pp. 131–132

35. Breuer, William B. *Hoodwinking Hitler*. Westport, Connecticut: Praeger Publishers, 1993, pp. 121–122

36. Ibid, pp. 120–130

37. Brown, Anthony Cave, *Bodyguard of Lies*. New York: Harper & Row, 1973, pp. 469–472

38. Ibid, Gawne, p. 17

39 Fox, Fred. *Digest of Operations 23rd Headquarters Special Troops Official History* (Regraded Unclassified- Sec Army per 203913)

40. William Shakespeare, Macbeth, Act 5, Scene 5

41. Interviews with Bernie Bluestein, 5 April and 12 July 2018

42. Courtesy, 2013 Plate of Peas Productions blog

43. Bluestein interview, 5 April 2018

44. Ibid, Digest of Operations, 23HQ Spec Troops 20391

45. Souter, Gerry. *The Burlington Zephyrs*. North Branch, Minnesota: Specialty Press, 2005, p. 88

46. Ibid, Gawne, pp. 70–73

47. Talty, Stephan. *Agent Garbo: the Brilliant, Eccentric Secret Agent*

who Tricked Hitler & Saved D-Day. Boston: Houghton Mifflin Harcourt, 2012, pp. 26–28

48. Ibid, pp. 48–50

49. Pujol, Juan with Nigel West. *Operation Garbo: The Personal Story of the Most Successful Double Agent of World War II.* New York: Random House, 1985, p. 81

50. Ibid, p. 84

51. Ibid, Pujol, p. 98

52 Ibid, Tally, pp. 187–89

53. Ibid, pp. 191–92

54. Ibid, pp. 194–96

55. Ibid, pp. 210–211

56. Ibid, pp. 226–28

57. Ibid Fox, *Digest of Operations 23rd Headquarters Special Troops*

58. Bluestein interview, 12 July 2018

59. Ibid, Gawne, pp. 50–51

60. NAAFI Public Relations Branch, *The Story of NAAFI,* 1 April, 1944

61. Trueman, C. N., The Falaise Pocket, historylearningsite.co.uk.

NOTE: Chapters 17–24: Unless otherwise noted, all references to training or operations in the ETO, 1944–45 are from *Digest of Operations 23rd Headquarters Special Troops Official History*

62. Ibid, Gawne, pp. 111–19

63. Bluestein interview, 5 April 2018

64. Atkinson, Rick. *The Guns at Last Light,* New York: Henry Holt & Co. 2013, p. 308

65. Bernie Bluestein interview, 12 July 2018

66. Ibid, Gawne, pp. 109–163 and Ambrose, Stephen. *Citizen Soldiers:*

The U.S. Army from the Normandy Beaches to the Bulge to the Surrender of Germany. New York: Simon and Schuster, 1997, pp. 157–159.

67. Bernie Bluestein interview, 12 July 2018.

68. Ibid, Atkinson, *Guns at Last Light*, pp. 416–419

69. Trewhitt, Philip A, *Armored Fighting Vehicles*, New York: B & N Publishing, 1999, p. 26.

70. C. Peter Chen, World War II Data Base, https://ww2db.com/battle_spec.php?battle_id=134

71. Bluestein interview, 12 July 2018

72. Ibid

73. Bluestein interview, 5 April 2018

74. Ibid, Gawne, pp. 237–245 and Davis, Jr., Franklin M., *Across the Rhine.* New York: Time Inc., 1980, pp. 78–83

75. Kneece, Jack. *Ghost Army of World War II.* Gretna, Louisiana: Pelican Publishing Company, Inc., 2001, p. 265

76. Ibid, p. 266

77. Bluestein interview, 5 April 2018

78. Bluestein interview, 12 July 2018

INDEX